THE WIND FARM SCAM

WITHDRAWN

THE WIND FARM SCAM

AN ECOLOGIST'S EVALUATION

John Etherington

STACEY
INTERNATIONAL

The Wind Farm Scam

STACEY INTERNATIONAL
128 Kensington Church Street
London W8 4BH
Tel: +44 (0)20 7221 7166; Fax: +44 (0)20 7792 9288
Email: info@stacey-international.co.uk
www.stacey-international.co.uk

ISBN: 978 1905299 83 6

CIP Data: A catalogue record for this book is available from the British Library

© Dr John Etherington 2009
Reprinted 2009
Reprinted 2010
Reprinted 2010

5 7 9 0 8 6 4

Printed in Turkey

CONTENTS

LIST OF TABLES AND FIGURES

Foreword

I owe John Etherington, the author of this book, a considerable debt. Over recent years he has given me invaluable technical guidance on one of the most extraordinary stories I have covered in all my decades as a journalist.

For me it all began back in 2002, just after Tony Blair had announced plans for a huge increase in the number of wind turbines to generate electricity in Britain, to meet targets set by the European Union in its bid to "fight climate change".

My eye was then caught by a report that Denmark, the country which had more wind turbines per head than any other in Europe, was reining back hard on building any more. It seemed they were not generating very much electricity, that what little they did produce had made Danish electricity the most expensive in Europe and that any savings in CO_2 emissions were virtually non-existent.

This seemed such a contradiction to the, then, still widespread belief that wind power provided a "free", "clean", "green" way to produce electricity – particularly since Mr Blair was now making it the centrepiece of his energy policy – that I decided to look into the facts behind it.

A friend put me on to Country Guardian, an internet site run from a cottage in Wales by Angela Kelly. She turned out to be a remarkable widow in her 70s, who has done more than anyone else in Britain to keep an ever wider circle of readers briefed on the facts about wind power. She put me onto one of her technical advisers, Dr Etherington, an academic scientist with a background in both energy and environmental issues. And it was he more than anyone else who opened my eyes to the extraordinary series of illusions on which this new political infatuation with wind energy was based.

Like most people at that time, I knew little about the practicalities of wind power. On visits to Cornwall, I had seen the array of relatively small wind turbines at Delabole, the first in Britain, and regarded them as little more than a rather picturesque curiosity. But as I went on a crash course in the hard facts behind wind energy – and for reasons which Dr Etherington lays out so methodically in this book – what a shock it turned out to be.

There are three particular reasons why this story is so shocking. The first is how astonishingly ineffective is the use of wind to generate electricity, above all because it blows so intermittently and unpredictably. This means that the actual amount of electricity it produces is derisory, barely a quarter as much as the owners of wind "farms" like to pretend or as our politicians have been fooled into believing. Between them, all the 2,400 wind turbines so far built in Britain generate, on the government's own figures, only a minute fraction of the electricity we need, just over 1.3 per cent. This is less than the output of a single medium-size conventional power station.

The second element which makes this shocking is that, far from being "free", generating energy from wind is horribly expensive, at least twice as costly as the electricity produced by conventional power stations. This means that the only reason developers are keen to build wind turbines is that they receive a series of huge hidden subsidies, often equivalent to 100 per cent or more of the cost of the electricity. These are paid for by all of us through our electricity bills. Dr Etherington, who explains in this book how this system works, describes how this makes wind-generated electricity arguably the most heavily subsidised commodity in history.

Still more shocking, however, is the immense environmental cost of wind energy. Not only do the owners of turbines vastly exaggerate any savings they make in CO_2 emissions (a single large new gas-fired power station, compared with a coal-fired power plant of similar output, saves more CO_2 than all our wind turbines put together), But as ever more giant wind turbines, as tall as 400 feet or more, march over many of the most beautiful, unspoiled landscapes of Britain, from the countryside of Devon to the hills of Wales, Cumbria and Northumberland to the moors, mountains and islands of Scotland, we are losing one of the most priceless natural assets our country possesses, on a scale for which our descendants will find it hard to forgive us.

This is not even to mention the increasingly well-quantified damage done by wind "farms" to wildlife, from birds to bats to the ecology of ancient peat bogs; let alone the environmental hell inflicted by noise and "flicker" on those who have to live near turbines forced through the planning process by increasingly arrogant and undemocratic government diktats.

For all these reasons, Dr Etherington and I have both called this tragic collective delusion "the Great Wind Scam". Earlier in life I spent some years exposing the colossal blunder which disfigured so many of Britain's cities in the 1960s with huge concrete tower blocks of council flats. At the time it was supposed that these were an answer to Britain's housing shortage, because these blocks enabled more people to be housed more cheaply on the same amount of ground. In fact those tower blocks were far more expensive to build than human-scale low-rise homes and they housed many fewer people. But they made a small number of people rich, at the expense of the millions who had to live in the monstrosities they had erected.

Eventually the obsession of our politicians with tower blocks was seen to be one of the greatest follies of the age. In time to come – it may be sooner than we think – the obsession with wind power will likewise come to be seen as an even greater folly. Few were quicker to recognise this and more effectively than John Etherington and his ally Angela Kelly of Country Guardian. The facts set out in this admirable book may help to explain why so many of us are in their debt.

Christopher Booker
May 2009

Preface

The mountains of Powys and Cardiganshire carry what from a distance look like a golgotha of gibbets. (Simon Jenkins. *The Times*, 15 February, 2002)

It is as if some malevolent creature from mythology had shed its spawn over the land, the brood twitching and writhing on the hilltops, the cliffs and even over the sea. At a wave of its wings it has bewitched the impressionable into belief that wild lands are somehow so bleak and featureless that they are improved – even beautified – by these winged monsters. Worse still, it has persuaded them that so much advantage is to be gained that we must open our farm gates, our parks and beaches for yet more flickering steel and plastic machines or we shall be doomed to a future with no electricity and global temperatures rising so sharply that life will become intolerable with wars fought for living-space and water, leaving a few survivors at the South Pole!

It all sounds so dramatic that it can hardly be true – or can it? In *The Wind Farm Scam* I set out to explore the truth or otherwise of this rather extreme view, starting from far back in the 1970s when I encountered my first tiny "wind turbines", one in the Irish Aran Islands and two others on the shores of Carmarthen Bay in Wales where the Central Electricity Board more correctly called them "aerogenerators".

But maybe it started before that? My paternal grandfather was a shipwright in the closing years of the age of sail and my father, starting life as a dockyard apprentice, became an electrical and mechanical engineer who, by the time he retired was head of a large technical college engineering department and a source of inspiration to me. My older brother was the first of our family ever to obtain a University degree – in Electrical Engineering from the Imperial College of Science and Technology, University of London. He worked for the Central Electricity Generating Board until its dissolution and so, by the time I obtained my PhD, also at Imperial College, I had been immersed up to my neck for several years in talk of heavy electrical engineering and all its ancillary industries.

It was an unexpectedly valuable honing of my skills as an environmental scientist – mostly to the credit of my father who was insatiably curious about every facet of science and speculated interminably about "received wisdom". He rightly imbued me with a lasting suspicion of "consensus" interpretation of science where it is not only out of place but a threat to the truth. I can only wish that he and my brother were still alive and continuing to advise me. I know beyond doubt that they would support my view that the wind monsters will do nothing useful for us, will spread environmental harm and above all have only one serious function – of minting money for the undeserving, aided and abetted by the uneducated.

My wife Sheena has been immensely supportive during the years that I have been abstracted, perhaps even obsessed by the need to expose the failings of this damaging industry. To her, my clever best friend, I owe more than I can say.

There is an immeasurable debt to many folk with whom I have corresponded during the past two decades. Above all I mention Angela Kelly of Country Guardian (CG) whose single-handed and self-effacing efforts have brought understanding to countless people in the battle to protect their local, national and international "backyards". The hysterical cries of "Nimby!" ['Not in my backyard!"] from the wind promoters rebound upon them – indeed, these Nimby campaigners are the new heroic defenders of the land. They need to be, when we have government ministers unashamedly lobbying for the wind power industry as did the Welsh Environment Minister when she wrote:

> You always get Nimbys right through the planning system
> but once people understand the contribution that
> renewable energy can make to keeping their power supply
> on and keeping the cost more reasonable I think we will
> be further down the road to winning the battle. (Renewable
> Energy News 151, 2008)

In late 2004 Country Guardian commissioned me as an independent consultant to write a revised version of *The Case Against Wind Farms* (CG website 2006 (countryguardian.net)), an undertaking that inspired and prepared the ground for much of this book.

There are countless others – too many to name. David "Botanist" Bellamy and Christopher Booker, who has kindly provided a foreword to this book, had the vision to ask me the right and sometimes very difficult questions. Answering them helped a lot. Alan Shaw, Derek Birkett and Paul Spare have enormously extended my education in power engineering and helped to debunk much of the ill-informed nonsense which is used to justify the wind power industry to gullible politicians and impressionable public. Mike Hall, Allan Tubb, Dave Bruce, Bob Graham and many others have helped with huge amounts of information and their ever-encouraging common sense.

Here at home in Wales stalwart defenders of our country such as Ioan Richard, Lyn Jenkins and Alun Richard fight relentlessly against the worst excesses of the wind power industry. Kaye Little, Elizabeth Morley and Peggy Liford deserve special mention for their role in the lost battle against the Cefn Croes wind farm high on the shoulder of Plynlimon in the Cambrian Mountains which involved me for the first time as more than just an interested spectator. David Insall has helped with discussion and played a part in the conception of this book. Mal Davies and Jan Moseley are particularly in my memory. They both did so much until losing their battles against ill-health. They were inspirations to all of us with their message "Never give up". I miss them greatly – and their help, more.

I also remember, with quite different feelings, former Department of Trade and Industry Energy Minister, Brian Wilson, who wrote:

> I also picked up the fascinating result of a survey by the British Wind Energy Association that 25 per cent of all the "anti-wind power" letters in newspapers throughout the UK over the last couple of years have been written by just 16 people – three of whom are now dead, presumably from overwork. (*West Highland Free Press*, 5 April, 2002)

An appalling comment about men who were the loved ones or friends of colleagues. A complaint to Prime Minister Blair concerning such a statement by a Minister of the Crown was not even acknowledged. This is the political attitude – "Wind power at all and every cost" – which has made me a campaigner rather than an interested analyst.

The battle over "tackling global warming", and the proposed ways and means taxes ordinary understanding. How can the average Jo in the street distinguish good from bad, genuine and informed concern for the environment from a callous and exploitive pursuit of a quick buck? In this book I have tried to give some answers, albeit from a biased premise that common sense and the reality of applied science is nearer the truth than the advertising spin of those who would sell wind power as the patent medicine for a malady which it cannot treat and which may not exist at all. If I manage to communicate that truth persuasively perhaps – just perhaps – it may make a difference.

My apologies to any helpers I have failed to name – there are just too many of you. I have no doubt made some mistakes – only he who does nothing, does not. Tell me about them and I will attempt to learn and correct. They are my mistakes, not those of all the kind friends who have helped me.

Terminology, units – Power and Energy

It is inevitable that many engineering and scientific terms appear, though I have tried to keep to everyday language where possible. Terms are explained when they first appear and measurements are given in SI (System International) units accompanied by everyday "translations" for clarity. Thus a wind speed of 15 metres per second (15 m/s) is also 34 miles per hour (34 mph) and, incidentally on the Beaufort scale, a "Near Gale".

The unit of electricity output (power) from a generator or consumption by a device is the watt (W). It is an instantaneous expression of rate of energy consumption or conversion, just as miles-per-hour is the instantaneous speed of a car. For convenience, multipliers are used to avoid huge written numbers. The consumption by an electric lamp is usually written in watts (W), that of a big machine in kilowatts (1,000 W = 1 kW) and the output of large generators in megawatts (1,000,000 W = 1 MW). Country wide consumption of electricity is measured in gigawatts (GW) and terawatts (TW); these respectively are 1,000 MW and 1,000,000 MW (note: all abbreviations use upper case letters apart from the kilo-multiplier which is a lower case "k").

Total energy use or output is expressed by multiplying the instantaneous power by time, thus a generator giving 1 MW of power, run for one hour, will give a total energy output of 1 MW x 1 h = 1 MWh (megawatt hour). A 1 kW lamp run for one hour will use 1 kWh which is also the Unit of consumption which appears on a domestic electricity bill. The use and misuse of these expressions causes endless confusion.

For convenience I shall henceforward refer to the need for instantly available electric power as "need for MW" – this would, for example, occur if many consumers simultaneously switched on an electric fire. Then there is the "need for MWh" – that is the sustained provision of electricity over a period of time, say to recharge hot water tanks. In the domestic milieu, need for kW or need for kWh is a more convenient measure as the average home uses only 4.7 MWh in a year.

Here and there in the text reference is made to baseload generation and load-following ability. The baseload of a generation-supply system is the continuous consumption level below which the system never falls between peaks. A power station providing baseload must be able to generate 24/7 for months without fail. Wind power cannot do this. Load-following supply is that which can be turned up and down to follow demand. Again because it is never guaranteed, wind cannot do this either.

Introduction

"He who refuses to do arithmetic is doomed to talk nonsense."
(John McCarthy, computer pioneer, Stanford University)

Electricity generated by modern industrial wind turbines has many failings, all of which can be traced back to the physical laws which govern air movement and limit the energy that can be extracted from the wind. The huge size of the machines which makes them so inappropriate in the countryside is also a consequence of those same physical laws.

Some of the biggest wind turbines on land are now almost 600 feet tall – about one and a half times the height of Salisbury Cathedral spire, the tallest in Britain, which Constable painted so many times. It is it is their huge size and constant movement which raises the ire of landscape protection groups and it is their visual impact on the countryside which influences the average person, if only because they see a potential effect on the value of their homes.

One of the Frequently Asked Questions on the British Wind Energy Association (BWEA)'s website is

> Why don't they make turbines that look like old fashioned windmills?

Well, that would need wind turbines to be a quarter or less of the present height and somehow avoid the mass-produced "plastic and steel" look, not to mention dispensing with the "aircraft propeller"! That the question has been asked at all is acknowledgement of a real visual problem, despite a page heading elsewhere on the BWEA website:

Wind Farms and Tourism. A valuable addition to the landscape.

The answer is that if the wind is to give significant amounts of power there is no option to these huge machines, because so little energy can be carried by moving air which is very light. The available energy from wind or water power is a product of the mass of air or water passing through the rotor per unit time. Doubling the circular area of a rotor doubles the amount of air or water which can pass through it. Air is about one 800th the density of water which is why a tiny old fashioned waterwheel mill could grind as much grain as a 100 foot traditional windmill. For the same power output, a windmill's sails need to encompass almost a thousand times the circular area of the equivalent waterwheel – a similar relationship exists between a modern hydroelectric turbine rotor and that of a wind turbine. This is because the energy harvested is, at a given air or water flow-rate, proportional to the mass of air passing through the rotor. It is an inevitable outcome of physical laws and powerful wind turbines can never grow smaller.

Really gigantic wind turbines like the 600 foot behemoths can generate 6 megawatts (MW) of power but only when it is very windy – a Beaufort scale "Near Gale" and about the wind speed at which our TV weather ladies start warning us about gusts and driving conditions. Six megawatts by the way is about half of one per cent of the power output of a large "real" power station – a pretty poor return for effort! If this optimum wind speed is halved to a comfortable breeze, the output will fall to much less than half of the maximum 6.0 MW – less than 1.0 MW. This is the consequence of another unchangeable physical law. The energy carried by a moving fluid such as water or air is proportional to the flow-rate cubed – that is halving the flow rate gives one eighth the available energy ($\frac{1}{2} \times \frac{1}{2} \times \frac{1}{2}$). We shall meet this in more detail later.

Weather forecasting as we all know to our cost is a thankless task and yet electricity supply systems have to be predictable so that generation can be kept instantaneously in balance with consumption (if not there is a loud "bang" and the lights go out). We have all heard that "tomorrow's winds will be near gale force" only to wake to a gentle breeze. Pity the owner of the much subsidised wind turbine whose income has swooped with the falling wind! Indeed because the owner cannot predict how much electricity he can generate tomorrow, he would not be able to sell at all in a competitive free market. It is only the compulsion to purchase renewable electricity imposed by governments on the distribution networks, and the consumer-sourced subsidies, which allow the wind power industry to exist at all.

The problem of unpredictable wind and unpredictable wind electricity supply arises from the chaotically turbulent nature of the atmosphere and the longer-term swirls of global weather systems. In many places, particularly the windward shores of large oceans, it is possible for weather fronts and large shifts of wind velocity to pass through the few hundred miles of ocean fringe in less than half a day and at other times anticyclones of colossal size may become stationary for days on end bringing cloudless, wind free hot weather in summer and similar but freezing cold conditions in winter. The North Atlantic coast of Europe is just such a place and it is here that the great wind farms of Denmark, Germany and the UK are situated.

Over the past three decades, wind power seems to have appeared from nowhere, to dominate the world of power generation. This is hardly because it provides a lot of electricity and yet it has become a source of vigorous support by extremists, public dissent and political coercion. Entering "wind power" in a Google search gives about 20 million hits (as I write)! And yet worldwide, wind provides just one or two per cent of power. Try a search for "electricity generation" and there are 1.5 million hits – a "spin disproportion" I think.

In the UK during 2007 wind power gave just 1.3% of our electricity compared with a total of 91% from fossil fuels and nuclear. Of the other renewable sources of power, hydroelectricity gave 1.2% and various forms of biomass combustion about 2.3%. Wind power has however grown very rapidly – more than sixfold in the UK, from less than 0.2% of supply in the late 1990s. With the exceptions of a few countries which have a huge hydroelectric resource or with unusually high reliance on nuclear power, these percentages and growth rates are more or less mirrored in many other western developed countries.

Why has there been such a growth in renewables and why should wind power have so outstripped other sources? The average person in the street could probably answer part of this question if they have absorbed the mantra which is repeated *ad nauseam* in the media which claim that renewable electricity:

1. can be generated without burning fossil fuel which is rapidly running out.
2. emits little or no carbon dioxide (CO_2) and so ameliorates man-made global warming.
3. will allow us to dispense with nuclear power which is supposedly dangerous.
4. will give us very cheap electricity because nature provides the power with no fuel-cost.
5. increases security of supply by avoiding reliance on imported fuel.

These reasons for exploiting renewables are in some cases untrue or are serious exaggerations of the truth. They camouflage the fact that the rush to renewables is more a matter of quick profit than about saving the world from self-inflicted disaster. The public at large is beginning to suspect this, but there is huge political inertia based on the fear that individuals or parties may be branded as "climate change deniers" with all the horrific undertones that phrase carries. Indeed extremists in the media have already proposed "Nuremberg type climate trials" for the deniers![1] There is little reason for politicians to fear such accusations for, as we shall see, even if every claim concerning global warming were correct there is not a hope that wind power could alter CO_2 emissions sufficiently to measurably alter the progress of warming. The huge growth of wind power compared with other renewables has happened because it is a relatively mature technology compared with more recent developments such as solar photovoltaic or wave-power, and also because several renewables are already near their limits of exploitation. For example the most productive hydroelectric sites have already been utilised, waste biomass is limited in availability and the land for dedicated biomass cultivation is needed for agriculture, thus its exploitation is forcing-up food prices or destroying biodiversity by taking virgin land. Biomass combustion does of course liberate CO_2 in similar quantities to fossil fuel and is thus only "carbon neutral" in the context of photosynthetic recycling. By comparison, wind and water power effectively produce no CO_2.

Nuclear power also produces next to no CO_2 but until very recently "green" activity has precluded even discussion of it as a greenhouse-free power source even though it can provide continuous huge output of base-load supply which wind cannot, and also with new PWR reactors will be able to load-follow which, again, wind cannot do.

The intention of this book is to highlight and justify reasons for rejecting wind power as a large scale source of electricity and of reducing carbon emission. In using the word "scam" in the title I shall draw down the anger of many environmentalists and green campaigners. However, a "scam" is often defined as "an attempt to swindle people which involves gaining their confidence." Exactly! The repeated reference to "tackling climate change" as a motivation for wind power, and the constant citation of the 1997 Kyoto treaty "targets" as justification is just such an attempt to gain public confidence. The spectre of climate change is being used as a scare-tactic to get people to buy wind power. This is the old quack-doctor trick – "Scare 'em to death and they'll buy anything". It will certainly be seen by history as a swindle supported by untruths and half-truths. I hope without too much exaggeration to "tell it as it is".

One of the first attempts to bring really large scale wind power to the UK was made in the late 1990s by the US Enron Corporation which collapsed in financial scandal in 2001. By that time the Kyoto Treaty was already coming into effect. A senior Enron employee gave a damning pre-Kyoto assessment in an internal memo, in which he wrote:

> If implemented, this agreement will do more to promote Enron's business than will almost any other regulatory initiative outside of restructuring of the energy and natural gas industries in Europe and the United States.[2]

The truth of this statement survived longer than the company which made it!

It does not escape the more cynically inclined "doubters" of wind power that some of the loudest voices in the development of the industry come from the same large companies which are responsible for excessive release of CO_2, the supposed reason for needing renewables in the first place, among them RWE-npower and E.ON UK. Indeed, the Prince of Wales's UK Corporate Leaders Group on Climate Change, which has said "deep and rapid" cuts were needed in greenhouse gas emissions, includes the executive officers of Tesco, BAA, Shell, and energy group E.ON – a fact which has prompted Greenpeace to describe the comment as "hypocrisy of a previously unknown magnitude". Now, with the world in the midst of the worst economic slump for decades, some of the world's leading investment banks have come together to discuss "cashing-in" on the carbon trading business.[3]

Pre-industrial wind power

Man first noticed and then harnessed the mechanical forces of nature as wind and water currents. A floating log in a flooded stream could not convey a clearer message, "This is how to move me". Carry a large leafy branch in a strong breeze and it practically shouts at you "I want to go this way – with the wind".

Paddled or poled boats appeared as very early human technology and by the British Bronze Age, sophisticated sewn plank boats existed, such as the seagoing Dover boat dating from

1500 BC, but long before this the Egyptian archaeological record preserved evidence of square-sailed boats as old as 3000 BC, and China may have used sail some centuries before this.

Such is human ingenuity that it did not take long to use the propulsive force of a sail to provide a stationary power source, driving a mill, a water-lift or perhaps a hammer. We have no clue how this happened but the running lines on a sail boat, coiled on a cylindrical belaying pin could have revealed the means of generating a turning force and at an informed guess, led to the first wooden pulleys. From these it is but a small leap of imagination to the sail-driven wind-shaft, but a leap which nevertheless took a millennium or more as the first vertical shaft windmills date from around the seventh century AD in Persia but the much commoner design today, horizontal shaft machines – the familiar windmill – were not developed until the tenth century.

Alongside the development of wind power, water also played its part and, where it was available, was preferred to wind. The power available from a moving liquid or gas is a direct function of its density, so, being 800 times denser than air, a relatively small waterwheel will do the same work as an enormous windmill of almost 1,000 times the circular area, as we saw above. By the seventeenth century much of the world's work was done by wind and water. The windmill on land had reached a high degree of sophistication and at sea, sailing vessels were a complex triumph of man's control of the elements. Some thousands of watermills are listed in the Domesday Book, but the windmill did not appear in Britain until the twelfth or thirteenth century.

By the time of Cobbett's *Rural Rides* in the early 1800s there were some 10,000 British windmills, but by the end of World War II almost all had been destroyed, dismantled or just abandoned. I remember one or two working mills in the 1940s and '50s but the stronger memory is of the ruined stumps of derelict windmills, two within a couple of miles of my childhood home in Kent.

The loss of the mills happened almost as if a contagious disease had swept the country clear of its former inhabitants, but it was not contagion, simply a logical succession to the convenience and cheapness of the invading steam engine. The engines won so quickly because wind does not blow all the time, and when it does blow it may not be hard enough, or it may be so hard that sailing vessels are wrecked or their rigging carried away while onshore, the sails of mills are destroyed or fire started by friction in "runaway" accidents. This unpredictable variability of wind and water, which killed the traditional mills, is a key fact to which I shall return later.

The modern wind power industry repeatedly cites the aesthetic appeal of the traditional mills as justification for the new generation of airfoil wind turbines – for example the turbine which has inexplicably been allowed above the iconic Glyndebourne Opera House in West Sussex will stand on an former site of a windmill, and much was made of this fact prior to the planning application. This totally misses the point that the comparison is of magnificent hand-crafted structures with mass-produced plastic, steel and concrete machines, not to mention that the average windmill was quarter the height of a large wind turbine and equivalent in landscape scale to churches, large barns and the trees of a semi-wooded landscape, a fact celebrated by several generations of landscape artists.

References and notes

1. David Roberts (2006), Grist online Magazine, in publicising George Monbiot's book *Heat*, wrote "When we've finally gotten serious about global warming, when the impacts are really hitting us and we're in a full worldwide scramble to minimize the damage, we should have war crimes trials for these bastards – some sort of climate Nuremberg." In a later issue Roberts was forced to a humble retraction: "My analogy to the Nuremberg trials was woefully inappropriate – nay, stupid. I retract it wholeheartedly."
    (http://gristmill.grist.org/story/2006/10/12/115734/52)
2. Christopher C. Hormer (25/4/2002) California Scheming.
    TechCentralStation (acknowledged to *Washington Post*).
3. *The Guardian*, (22 October, 2008) Investment banks meet in London to discuss how they can "cash in" on carbon.

1   Wind turbines

Like Concorde, a modern wind turbine is a remarkable feat of ingenuity and it is hardly surprising to find such outer limits of civil engineering described as elegant – even beautiful. Many of us felt the same about Concorde, a magnificent proof of Anglo-French techno-agreement. It should have been at the two billion it cost the taxpayers (which would have been twenty at today's prices). As with Concorde there should be a couple of wind turbines in a museum. (Private email, 2006)

Windmills and airfoils. A traditional windmill has sails which are more or less flat and tilted longitudinally so that wind energy is converted to rotary motion, the blade being effectively pushed out of the way by air pressure. The modern wind turbine (or more correctly "aerogenerator") is more sophisticated, having an airfoil rotor which resembles a giant aircraft propeller. As air passes over the wing-like rotor blade a combination of air-pressure change and frictional forces generates lift and drag, the resultant of which causes rotation and much more efficiently harvests the kinetic energy of the wind. The development of the aircraft industry between the world wars led substantial research into the complex aerodynamic behaviour of airfoils (propellers and wings) and to the development of control systems such as pitch regulation in which the whole or part of the blade of a propeller may be rotated on its longitudinal axis to vary energy exchange with the surrounding air.

Types of wind turbine. The commonest design of wind turbine is a three-bladed airfoil propeller mounted on a horizontal axle, the wind shaft, which drives a gearbox (to increase revolution speed)

Table 1.1 Wind turbines. Size and technical characteristics.

Size	Very large	Large	Small (farm scale)	Small (domestic)
Example – Manufacturer & model	Enercon E 112 (Notes 1 & 2)	Vestas V 80 (Note 3)	Proven WT 15000	Windsave 1000 (Note 4)
Installed capacity	4.5 - 6.0 MW	2.0 MW	15 kW	1.25 kW
Rotor diameter m (feet)	114 (374)	80 (262)	9 (29.5)	1.75 (5.7)
Total max height to blade tip m (feet)	198 (650)	140 (459)		
Rotor speed r.p.m.	Variable, 8 - 13	Variable, 9 - 19		
Blade tip speed m/s (mph)	48 - 78 (112-175)	38-80 (84-176)		
Cut in wind speed m/s (mph)	2.5 (5.6)	4 (9)	2.5 (5.6)	3.5 - 5.0 (7.8-11)
Peak output wind speed m/s (mph)	12 (27)	15 (34)	12 (27)	
Cut out wind speed m/s (mph)	28-34 (63-76)	25 (56)	Above 12 (27) self-furling	14-15 (31-34)

1. Gearless turbine – direct drive to generator. Variable pitch control.
2. Enercon is not supplying wind turbines to offshore projects as the costs and risks of offshore wind farms outweigh the alternative while the demand for onshore wind turbines continues (as of 2008).
3. Gearbox variable speed. Variable pitch control.
4. *Which* magazine (September, 2008): "During the four month period when the wind around the tester's home was at its strongest, the turbine generated a net amount of just 1.8 kilowatt hours of power – equal to 45 minutes of ironing. The wind turbines were also noisy. Our tester's children were disturbed by a ghostly humming at night . . . We can't recommend turbines to anyone living in a built-up environment – considering the purchase cost, planning issues and the small amount of energy produced."

and is in turn coupled to an electricity generator which may be either a DC generator or an AC alternator. The blade mounting is via a hub assembly which, in sophisticated machines, includes mechanism for blade pitch control. The windshaft-gearbox-generator assembly is contained in a weather protective nacelle mounted on the top of a tower, nowadays usually a cylindrical steel structure (Fig 1.1). As with traditional windmills there must usually be a means of pointing the windshaft toward the wind, typically a yaw motor which rotates the whole nacelle on a yaw-bearing atop the tower.

Wind turbines may range from rooftop machines just a few metres in total height with an output rarely exceeding 10 kilowatts (kW) to giant structures of total height 150m to 180m (500 to 600 feet) and output reaching five megawatts (MW) or more in high wind (Table 1.1).

Occasional variants of this design are two-bladed and four-bladed machines and, increasingly, wind turbines without the troublesome gearbox but having a direct drive from the windshaft to a large diameter alternator in which permanent magnets mounted around the full diameter of the nacelle act as a ring generator. Virtually all wind turbines today are "upwind" designs with the rotor to windward of the tower, as opposed to "downwind" machines with the rotor in the wind-shadow of the tower which caused additional noise from turbulence and potential stress-damage to rotor and bearings.

Horizontal axis wind turbines are often referred to as HAWTs but during the more than century-long development of wind power, attempts have also been made to introduce vertical axis wind turbines (VAWTs) which have the design advantage of not needing to be yawed into the wind. Despite this, the VAWT design has never been a very successful competitor in the industry though small rooftop VAWTs are still marketed.

Components of a wind turbine

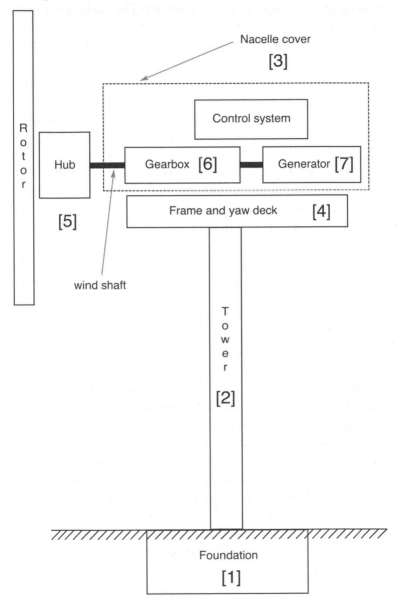

1.1   Schematic diagram. Horizontal axis wind turbine.

Foundation [1]. A diversity of foundation designs are used with the primary purpose of resisting the tilting stress imposed by wind on the rotor and tower. This has not always been successful and there have been occasional accidents in which the machines have literally blown over, tipping the foundation block like the roots of a gale-felled tree. The commonest onshore design is the simple concrete block, square, polygonal or circular in plan, several metres deep and reinforced with steel bars in the upper part. A published foundation design for a 3 MW Vestas V90 machine comprises a reinforced concrete square stability plate weighted by a deep layer of aggregate totalling in excess of 1,000 cubic metres and containing perhaps 1,600 tonnes of aggregate and 200 tonnes of cement.

Depending on bottom conditions, offshore turbines may be mounted on a tubular monopile driven to a substantial depth in the seabed or a caisson may be sunk to the sea bottom and filled with crushed rock aggregate providing a gravity foundation. The former involves little environmental disturbance other than the pile-driving operation but a gravity caisson may need as much structural material as is required for a block foundation on land.

Tower [2]. Most machines now being built have a slightly tapered tubular steel tower fabricated from sections welded or bolted together during construction. Internally it houses the drop-cables from the generator, other necessary connections and access arrangements for maintenance staff. Older and smaller machines have been mounted on lattice-girder towers and occasionally guyed towers. A two or three megawatt machine tower will be some three to four metres in diameter at the base, up to 100 m in height and several hundred tonnes in weight.

Nacelle [3] and machine platform [4]. The drive-train and generator of the turbine are enclosed in a weather-protective enclosure, the nacelle, which on a big machine is topped by a platform allowing helicopter access by maintenance staff – indeed the only access possible for much of the time offshore. The base of the nacelle provides a rigid platform which carries the weight of drive-train and generator and provides mounting for the major bearings of the wind shaft which have to resist huge stresses from the thirty tonnes or more of the rotor.

Yaw facility. Traditional tower-mills and smock-mills were fitted with a fan-tail rotor which kept its sails facing the wind by operating a circular rack and pinion device that rotated the whole mill cap when the wind was not parallel to the plane of the fan-tail. The yaw motor and wind sensor of a wind turbine do exactly the same job but require a great deal more power to counteract the "gyroscopic" force of the huge rotor and to avoid damage from this force by yawing too fast. Yawing can impose powerful bending forces on the rotor blades, their roots in the hub and on the wind-shaft and bearings. Usually the yaw motor causes the rotation of the entire machine platform and nacelle. There must also be a non-tangle provision for the drop-cables from the rotor down the tower to ground level.

Rotor, hub and windshaft [5]. The rotor-blade roots are bolted into the hub on the outer end of a horizontal windshaft of which the weight and bending forces are born by the rigid floor platform of the nacelle. The rotor of a three-bladed turbine is similar in design to a giant aircraft propeller with hydraulic or electromagnetic controls for blade pitch control and other mechanisms such as air-brakes which are usually a pitchable tip to the blade. Whole-blade pitch control, as well as allowing variation of the wind energy converted, may also provide air-braking. Embedded within the composite metal, fibreglass and synthetic resin blades are lightning conductors with contacts to the fixed conductor leading to an earth point at the foot of the tower.

Gearbox [6]. The inner end of the windshaft is coupled to a gearbox which steps-up the slow rotation of the rotor (typically 10 to 30 rpm) to the much higher speed necessary for AC generation. The slowly rotating, high torque power of the rotor is converted to high speed, low torque power needed by the generator, usually 3,000 rpm for 50 Hz AC output.

Generator(s) [7]. Wind turbine alternators (AC generators) may be either synchronous or asynchronous and with direct or indirect grid connection. Directly connected alternators are coupled directly to the AC distribution network (usually 3-phase). For indirectly connected machines, the voltage, frequency and other characteristics are processed by power-electronic devices which adjust the wind-feed to match that of the network (more in Chapter 2). With an asynchronous alternator this occurs automatically.

The commonest type of industrial wind turbine alternator is asynchronous, and the power generated is usually 690 V, three-phase AC which is passed to a transformer to raise the voltage to somewhere between 11,000 and 33,000 volts (UK local distribution network voltages). Most wind turbines work at a frequency of 50 Hz, the same as UK mains supply frequency (or 60 Hz in the US).

Wind and energy

Two factors govern the energy which can be converted by a wind turbine. Firstly, the work which can theoretically be done by the wind is a cubic function of wind speed – simply expressed, a doubling of wind speed giving eight times the useful energy (Fig 1.2). Secondly the energy which can be harvested by a wind rotor is proportional to its swept area and so a doubling of the swept area doubles the energy turning the wind shaft and alternator. Because the area of a circle is πr^2, a relatively small increase in rotor diameter will give substantial extra output (Fig 1.3).

The cubic law dictates that, as wind speed rises the turbine rotor will soon absorb so much energy that torque or rotational velocity may become hazardously large – indeed, damage to blades in high wind is one of the commonest wind turbine accidents. Modern wind turbines extend the range of wind speed in which they may

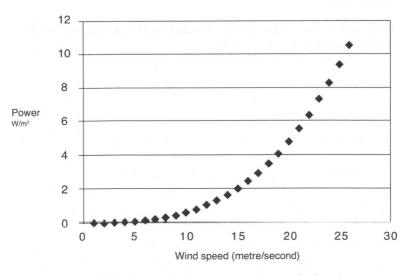

1.2 Power available from a 1.0 m² cross sectional area cylinder of moving air (wind) at air speeds of up to 30 m/s. Note that big wind turbines have a rotor area tens of thousands of times this and are able to harvest up to 30% to 50% of this power flow.

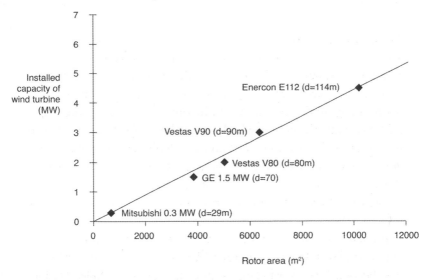

1.3 Relationship of wind turbine installed capacity (maximum output) to rotor area (solid line). Identified examples are plotted. Note large change of capacity for a relatively small change of diameter (d).

safely operate by utilising passive or active variation of the aerodynamic behaviour of the blades. The consequence is that the actual conversion of kinetic wind energy to electricity shown in Fig 1.4 is rather different from the energy content relationship of Fig 1.2. The difference in shape of the two curves in these graphs of energy available and actual electricity yield is a consequence of the alternator reaching its maximum output and then the aerodynamic design of the wind rotor blades allowing spillage of wind energy to avoid overloading.

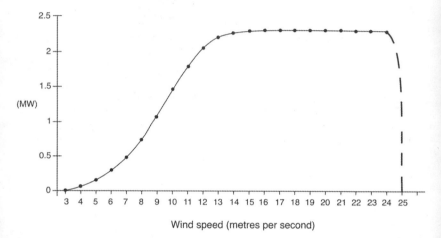

Wind speed (metres per second)

1.4 Typical power curve relating wind speed to electrical output. Data for a Bonus turbine (broken section at and above cut-out speed inserted by author). There is negligible generation below 5 m/s; peak output is not reached until 15 m/s (Beaufort 7 – Near Gale) and at 25 m/s the turbine is shut down for safety.

The area relationship with energy harvest and cubic relationship with wind speed are not just a matter of academic interest but have implications for all aspects of wind power from the size and visual impact of the machines in the landscape to the huge problems of integrating intermittently variable output into a distribution system which we have seen must maintain instantaneous and close-tolerance balance of generation versus consumption.

Passive – Stall Controlled Wind Turbines. These have the rotor blades bolted into the hub at a fixed angle but the geometry of the rotor blade profile is designed so that when the wind speed becomes too high, it creates turbulence on the side of the rotor blade which is not facing the wind, thus stalling the airflow and reducing the force rotating the blades. The aerodynamic design of the blade allows stall to extend progressively along the blade with rising wind so that less torque is transmitted to the rotor which is thus protected from overload, allowing generation to continue at higher wind speeds.

Active – Pitch Controlled Wind Turbines. The computer controlling turbine function constantly monitors power output and if it becomes too high, signals the blade pitch mechanism which immediately pitches the rotor blades slightly out of the wind. This involves rotation of the whole blade round its longitudinal axis usually by a hydraulic mechanism. The process is analogous to the furling of sails on a boat to reduce speed and protect running gear. The blades turn back into the wind whenever the wind drops again thus closely regulating output and the stresses to which the turbine is exposed.

Active – Stall Controlled Wind Turbines. An increasing number of larger wind turbines are being fitted with active stall power control which resembles pitch control as they have rotatable blades. When the machine reaches its rated power, if the generator is about to be overloaded, the machine will pitch its blades in the opposite direction from that of a pitch controlled machine. This increases the angle of attack of the rotor blades and spills the excess wind energy. One of the advantages of active stall is that power output can be controlled more accurately than with passive stall, so as to avoid overshooting the rated power of the machine in gusts of wind. Another advantage is that the machine runs at close to rated power at all high wind speeds, unlike passive stall turbines which lose some power at the highest tolerable wind speeds.

Unfamiliar terms

Load Factor (Capacity factor in the US). Any power generating unit whether thermal power station, wind turbine or hydroelectric generator cannot always produce maximum output, and may produce no electricity if it is shut down for service, has no fuel or there is no wind. The load factor is "The ratio of the electricity generated by a unit during a given period of time, to the energy it would have generated had it run continuously at maximum capacity for that period." Load factors are usually calculated as per cent per year but may be calculated for other periods of time. They must be compared only for the same base period and starting at the same point in time (e.g. January to December).

Installed capacity (MW or kW) is the maximum output of a wind turbine at optimum wind speed (or output of a conventional generator at full throttle). Multiplying the installed capacity by the load factor gives the average power yield over the time period used.

2   Wind-generated energy

The wind sprang up and broke the bells – Swinging between life and death   (TS Eliot)

What the UK government proposes

The scale of development required by government targets for renewable generation and saving of carbon dioxide emission are substantial. In January 2000 government announced its aim for renewables to supply 10% of UK electricity in 2010, "subject to the costs being acceptable to the consumer".[1]

The consequent target figure was 39 TWh/y which was 10% of predicted UK power generation based on the forecast of a total electricity production of 371–390 TWh/y in 2010. About 75% will have to be wind power so this would need 29.3 TWh/y or an average running wind power generation of 3,339 MW. Assuming a load factor of 30% this would require 11,130 MW, equivalent to more than 5,500 two MW-turbines.

However, to introduce a bit of harsh reality, the Department of Business, Enterprise and Regulatory Reforms (DBERR's) figure for wind power production in 2007, was 5.27 TWh[2] so the 2010 target is already beyond reach despite the 1,800 or so turbines we had in 2007 (albeit smaller than 2 MW). Further targets, conveniently re-christened "aspirations", exist for 2020 with a staging point at 2015.

Since the 2003 White Paper, political enthusiasm for wind power has grown apace, probably because the truth has dawned that biomass, wave energy and possibly even tidal power are unlikely to provide significant carbon emission savings, at least by 2020, if at all. It is also obvious that the raising of the sights for wind power also stemmed from the EU 2020 target for all energy production of 20%. Prime Minister Blair signed-up to this EU target as his last act of power at a March 2007 meeting of the 27 Prime Ministers of the EU. The feasibility of this target is further discussed in Chapter 10. Meeting it would require the proportion of electricity generation from wind power to increase from less than 2% now, to maybe 35% by 2020".[3] This would require a greatly increased installed capacity of 35,000 MW (17,500 2-MW turbines).

The rapidly expanding "aspiration" is illustrated by Government's plans to build an additional 33 GW of offshore and 14 GW of onshore wind capacity by 2020, announced in 2007. This is a total in the region of 50 GW (about 25,000 2-MW turbines) with an average output of perhaps 15 GW, varying with the vagary of wind between zero and 50 GW, which exceeds the current average generation for the whole UK and will impose an enormous and possibly insoluble problem of backup (see Chapter 5).

A brief history

Why has wind power generation arrived so suddenly on the scene – or has it? This may be more a matter of perception than fact. As we saw in the Introduction, windmills have harnessed natural energy for more than a millennium, powering cereal mills, moving water and taking the slavery out of large scale wood- and metal-working. It is hardly surprising that once electro-magnetic induction was understood following Michael Faraday's work in the early nineteenth century, and the first rotary DC and AC generators were built, someone would soon think of driving them with a wind powered rotor.

In the US, Charles Brush built a wind powered generator in 1888 and in the years that followed, small wind electric generators became widespread. The most well known was the Jacobs machine which made the step forward from the flat sail-blade of the classic windmill, to a rotor with three airfoil shaped blades, similar to the commonest configuration today, the horizontal axis wind turbine. Jacobs machines were marketed as residential power sources and came as a package which included a battery storage system – a significant fact to which we shall return.

Development of wind turbines in the US came to a standstill in the 1930s when rural electrification programmes brought "mains" electricity to even relatively remote communities. Such supplies were much more convenient and considerably cheaper than a troublesome windmill. However, for applications where intermittent operation was not a problem, such as pumping water, metal bladed "fan mills" were widely installed during these years. Several million of such machines were built in the US on remote farms with no electricity supply, and some remain in use today.

What might have happened in the US had cabled electricity not been adopted and fossil fuels not been so cheap? Very large wind turbines had first appeared at this time, for example a modern looking three-bladed 1.25 megawatt (MW) machine was installed in Vermont at Grandpa's Knob in the late 1930s and intermittently fed electricity into the local power system during the 1940s. The project was abandoned in 1945 after the rotor was damaged in high wind. Blade failures, right down to the present day, remain the commonest cause of damage to wind turbines despite the introduction of composite materials including fibreglass- or carbon fibre-reinforced resin polymers.

Development of large wind turbines did not really restart until the latter part of the twentieth century. The resurrection of wind power during the past two or three decades was based on the perception of need coupled with the greater ease of linkage to an AC power system conferred by solid state and computerised control systems. Continuous research into the aerodynamics of airfoils, stimulated by the aircraft industry in the twentieth century had also permitted the building of much more efficient and controllable rotors incorporating pitch control and movable control-surfaces which allow air-braking and regulation of energy capture.

The perceived need arose with the wide acceptance of belief in CO_2-driven climatic warming in the 1980s which provided a motivation for reducing fossil fuel use and controlling carbon dioxide emission. This motivation was in part deliberately cultivated and led to the formulation of the Kyoto protocol and the establishment of the Intergovernmental Panel on Climate Change (IPCC). The main switch to renewable development was finally thrown when various subsidies and tax breaks for "green" electricity became available world-wide, in response to powerful lobbying by well intentioned green campaigners and less altruistic pressure from the multinational power companies. As we shall see, nothing attracts entrepreneurs more than a free handout!

Wind speed, energy and height

When wind blows over land or water, frictional drag reduces its speed to zero at the surface. The speed increases with height until at some distance above the surface it is no longer significantly slowed. This change of wind speed with height is the "vertical wind shear". The depth of the wind shear zone is governed by the "surface roughness". A water surface has minimal surface roughness compared with, say, a land surface of trees and bushes, whilst a cityscape of mixed tall and short buildings, or rough rocky landscapes represent the upper extreme of roughness.

Low surface roughness causes only slight wind shear whilst the roughest of surfaces may influence wind speed to several hundred metres in height (Fig 2.1). This has implications for wind turbine engineering. For best performance an airfoil needs to be exposed to uniform air flow – in other words high enough to be out of the main shear zone. Over the sea, the wind speed does not change very much with the hub-height of the wind turbine and low towers of perhaps 0.75 times the rotor diameter may be used, compared with towers on land which have to be equal to or taller than the rotor diameter to lift it above the zone of substantial shear.

Steep gradients of wind shear also expose the rotor to unbalanced forces as the blades sweep through uppermost and lowermost positions. Because the kinetic energy of wind is related to speed by a cubic relationship (see below) there may be a very substantial unbalance which is responsible for fatigue failure of

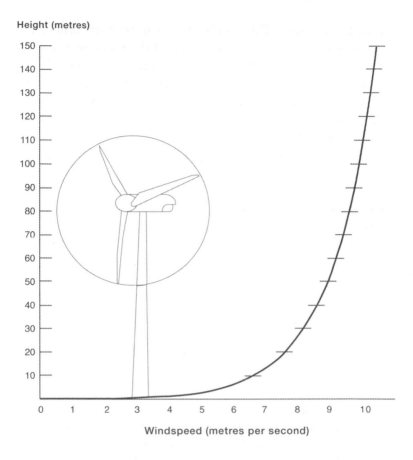

Height (metres)

Windspeed (metres per second)

2.1 Wind speed profile with height based on a wind of 10 m/s at 100 m and a roughness coefficient of 0.1 (Danish Wind Industry Association (DWIA) calculator). The illustrated turbine is tall enough for its rotor to be above the zone of greatest change.

blade-roots and wind-shaft bearings. The difference in wind shear between the highest and lowest blade-tip positions also creates an unbalanced source of aerodynamic noise which is partly responsible for the pulsing sound which causes complaint from those who live near wind turbines (See Chapter 7).

Wind speed geography

Today the wind is blowing. Tomorrow it won't be and indeed it may have dropped in a couple of hours. Sometimes it blows at a very low wind speed for weeks on end. A gale may move across the country in a few hours, followed by calm, possibly with repeat performances for a week or more.

In the UK there is a slight preponderance of winds from the southwest but a fairly high probability of winds from most other compass points. Wind turbines in general have to include an expensive yaw facility to allow the rotor to be turned toward the wind, though in some other countries and situations the prevailing wind may be so strongly biased to one compass point that this is unnecessary.

In the UK and indeed across the whole of northern Europe there is a strong auto-correlation between wind speeds and directions across very wide areas. In other words because of the large size of weather systems all of the wind farms in north Europe quite often behave similarly. When it is calm in my home country of Wales, an anticyclone may be stationary over northern Europe so that England and Scotland may also experience day after day of calm, either in hot summer weather and also in very cold mid-winter conditions.

Long persistence of wind-free or low wind conditions is one meteorological circumstance that wind power has to cope with whilst the other is the rapid transit of weather fronts across large land areas. In the UK it is not uncommon for wind speed to shift from near zero to near gale force or back in a matter of a few hours.

The short term shifts in wind which we interpret as part of our weather may be averaged over the years as the wind climate, as for example the geographical distribution of mean wind speed. Fig 2.2 shows the mean wind speed mapped in zones separated by 1 m/s for northern Europe, making it immediately apparent why most of the wind farms are on the Atlantic and North Sea coasts with more toward the north.

Mapped wind power is available at a much finer scale from BERR allowing wind speed to be assessed at several heights within

Fig 2.2 Distribution of mean wind speed in the British Isles.

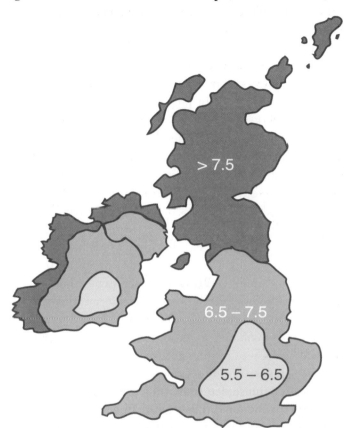

Light coloured zone is 5.6 to 6.6 m/s, increasing to more than 7.5 m/s in the far north and west. Source: European Wind Atlas. Troen and Peterson (1991).

each km-square of the UK Ordnance Survey national grid by entry of a four figure map reference into the database at http://www.berr.gov.uk/whatwedo/energy/sources/renewables/explai ned/wind/windspeed-database/page27326.html . Table 2.1 gives an example, the first for Stornoway on the Isle of Lewis in the Outer Hebrides where the largest wind farm in Europe was proposed, but rejected in planning and the second for West London where at least one politician notably installed a wind turbine on his home.

Table 2.1 Average wind speeds at three heights on an offshore Scottish island and in the shelter of a London suburb.

	Isle of Lewis			North Kensington		
Height	45 m	25 m	10 m	45 m	25 m	10 m
Mean m/s	9.0-10.0	8.2-9.6	7.5-9.0	6.0-6.1	5.7-5.5	4.8-4.9

The wind speed at 45 m on Lewis is about twice that at 10 m in London. The cubic relationship would give eight times the energy density available to a big turbine at the Scottish site compared with a roof-turbine in London. Building-mounted wind turbines are rarely a good investment.

It should be noted that average wind speed can be misleading – two days of a steady strong wind would give the same average wind speed as one day of gale and one of calm, the latter permitting no generation (2-day load factor 0%) but the former a 2-day load factor of 100%. Because of the cubic relationship of energy with speed the average electrical output may be very variable related to average speed. For this reason the wind speed data given in Fig 2.2 can only be approximations and use of the BERR database no more than a guide to suitability. It is usual for a developer to monitor wind speeds at a number of heights on a proposed site before proceeding with a wind power scheme.

Much more remains to be said about wind power and the weather it has to cope with. This is made much clearer by looking at actual power generating records (see Chapter 3).

Wind, energy and electricity generation

The energy carried by wind is as we have seen, related to the cube of its speed (thus doubling the speed it represents [2x2x2] i.e. eight times the energy content). Also, the energy which can be extracted is proportional to the mass of air passing through a wind turbine rotor, so doubling the swept area of the rotor doubles the energy available. As with most theoretical relationships matters are rather more complicated when we look at the behaviour of real machines.

No device which converts one form of energy to another is 100% efficient. Thus conversion of the kinetic power of wind to electricity, or the turning of chemical energy in fuel to mechanical work, involves losses. "Efficiency" in this context means the proportion of energy in one form which is converted to the other and the losses appear as heat which is dispersed to the environment during the process and as fuel wastage through poor combustion control.

In the case of a wind turbine not much energy is lost as friction-generated heat but wastage of the wind "fuel" is inevitable. The conversion of wind energy to electricity slows down the air stream as it passes through the rotor. To extract all the energy would slow the wind to a standstill and the rotor would stop. For a wind turbine to operate, some air must pass through the rotor and the physical laws which govern this aerodynamic fact dictate that no more than about 59% of the wind energy can be extracted by an air-rotor. This is called the Betz limit, named after the discoverer of the relationship.

In real life the best that can be achieved by big wind turbines is up to about 50% efficiency but once losses in the drive-train and alternator are added, the overall efficiency is around 30% or less, which is similar to the fuel efficiency of thermal power stations which typically run at 35% to 45% efficiency and use cooling-water to discharge surplus heat to rivers, sea or atmosphere. The efficiency may be somewhat increased if the hot water can be used for area heating or desalination but no more mechanical work can be extracted.

We have to be a bit careful about words then. It is often written that wind turbines are "inefficient" because they lose generating capacity when the wind drops. This is not a correct use of the word. A wind turbine without wind is equivalent to a car with no fuel. You would not say your car was "inefficient" when you carelessly run out of petrol! What is really meant is that wind turbines are ineffective because they frequently cannot run at all, and for much of the time generate far less than maximum output. These failures are no more predictable than weather forecasts. They pose many problems for the integration of wind with other power and reduce the marketability of the output.

How much wind – how much energy?

The energy content of the wind is so small at low wind speeds that no useful work is available below about 3 m to 5 m per second (7-11 mph; c. Beaufort 3). Above that speed energy content begins to increase substantially because of the cubic power relationship as we saw in Chapter 1 (Fig 1.2). Most wind turbines generate between this low speed limit and up to about 25 m/s (56 mph; c. Beaufort 9) when they shut down for safety. At very low wind speeds there is no output from a wind turbine as its rotor will be aerodynamically stalled and may be secured with a parking brake. There is no point in wearing out mainshaft bearings or yaw-drives for no purpose, or as happened on 16 August, 2002 in Denmark, consuming more electricity for keeping the machines facing the wind than the country's turbines generated.[4] As the wind speed increases it approaches the cut-in velocity (see Table 1.1), the brake is taken off and the rotor allowed to gather speed in the wind. For some wind turbines this starting-up process may need the alternator to be operated as a motor using electricity from the network to drive the rotor up to the necessary speed for operating the alternator at correct voltage output and AC synchronisation characteristics.

The increasing but low wind speed initially allows the electricity yield to follow closely the cubic energy function but in the mid-range of wind speed the pick-up of electricity output does not keep pace with energy availability necessitating aerodynamic spillage of wind, either by active operation of blade pitch control or passive stall regulation (Chapter 1). If this did not happen the rotor would rapidly go over-speed, possibly to destruction.

In the region of 15 m/s (34 mph; c. Beaufort 7 – Near Gale) the alternator reaches its maximum output capacity and the rising graph reaches a horizontal plateau extending to about 25 m/s, the shut-down limit. To prevent damage to the rotor it must at this wind speed be pitch regulated into a fully stalled position with the blades turning through about 90 degrees on the longitudinal axis so that virtually no wind energy is harvested. In the case of passively regulated machines (without pitch control), if the progressive aerodynamic stall regulation is insufficient to prevent overload, the rotor must be yawed away from the wind.

It is significant for the integration of wind power that wind velocity may vary rapidly and to a quite large degree. If this variation is within the high sensitivity cubic-response zone between cut-in and rated capacity wind speed the impact on electric power output may be enormous. The two vertical bars in Fig 2.3 indicate the effect of a plus or minus 1.0 m/s error in forecasting a 10 m/s wind speed. The power output for this 2.25

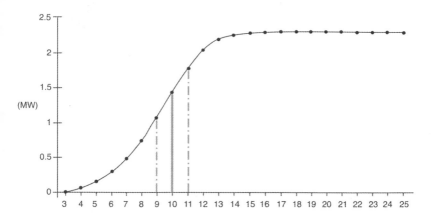

Fig 2.3   Sensitivity of forecast generation to inaccuracy of forecasting. The heavy vertical line indicates the expected generation at a wind speed of 10 m/s. A deviation of plus or minus 10% shifts actual generation within the limits shown by the two broken vertical lines. Because of the cubic relationship the power generation swings by some 50% of maximum for this overall 20% error of forecast.

MW turbine may vary by about 1.0 MW between the + and – limits so a shift of a moderate wind speed by 2 m/s (about 20%) causes generation to swing by some 50% of maximum. Wind changes of this order are frequent.

Such lurches of individual turbine output will tend to cancel each other out – not all machines on a site will experience a gust or lull simultaneously. However longer term shifts in wind speed caused by rapid travel of weather systems may frequently change the entire output of large areas by a very substantial proportion of average output as we shall see in the next chapter.

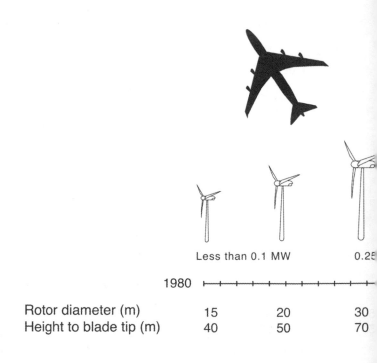

Less than 0.1 MW   0.25

1980

| Rotor diameter (m) | 15 | 20 | 30 |
| Height to blade tip (m) | 40 | 50 | 70 |

Fig 2.4   The growth with time of wind turbine rotor diameter, height and installed capacity. Silhouette is a Boeing 747 "jumbo" for size comparison.

The growth of wind turbines

In 1991 when the first commercial wind farm became operational in the UK, the 400 kW Vestas machines at Delabole in Cornwall appeared enormous. Now, 17 years later, the present owner, Good Energy, wants to replace the existing ten 50 m (164 ft) turbines with c. 130 m (426 ft) machines. This height is now about the industry standard in this country and represents 2.0 MW to 3.0 MW installed capacity with a rotor diameter of 80 m or more. The largest onshore wind turbines in Europe are several Enercon E112s in Germany. These are up to 198 m to blade-tip (650 feet), according to tower-height, with an installed capacity of between

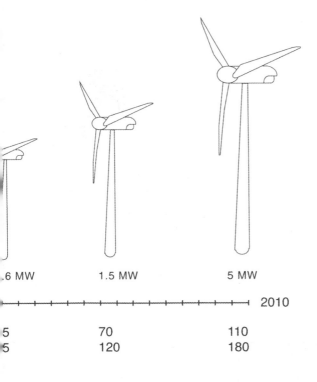

.6 MW	1.5 MW	5 MW

2010

| 5 | 70 | 110 |
| 5 | 120 | 180 |

4.5 and 6.0 MW. In the context of claims by developers and the WEAs that the life of a wind farm is 25 years, it is interesting that proposals such as this one at Delabole, for re-powering, are ensuring that replacement is well before this age. Why is it happening?

It is a reflection of the second of those unbeatable physical laws. The energy harvested by a wind turbine rotor is proportional to the mass of air passing through the rotor. Doubling the swept area of the rotor-circle doubles the amount of air which can pass and thus twice as much energy is captured. Numerically the energy available is proportional to the swept area and thus proportional to the square of the diameter because the area is π x (half diameter)^2.

Again this is another of those paper relationships which does not quite fit with actual performance. This is a logical consequence of the use of pitch regulation or passive aerodynamic spillage to regulate energy harvest. Many turbine designers have attempted to use such controls to tweak the performance of wind turbines within the valuable wind-speed versus yield range but essentially this can only make a minor difference. If the wind "farmer" wants a lot more electricity from his machine the rotor has to be much bigger and consequently the tower much taller, to the dismay of landscape protectionists.

Re-powering with bigger turbines might be looked upon as obtaining more electricity from the same area of wind farm but for a number of fundamental physical reasons this is unlikely to be true. As air passes through a wind rotor it is not only slowed but some energy is also lost in creating turbulence, a stream of vortices, rotating swirls of air extending downwind, spreading laterally from the turbine and commonly called a "wake". If another turbine is in the airstream affected by this wake it will also lose performance and for this reason it has been more or less a rule of thumb that turbines should be spaced at ten rotor diameters parallel to the prevailing wind and a little less at right angles to this direction. The consequence is that, as turbines grow, so their spacing also has to increase for optimum performance. There is evidence that 10 diameters may be far from sufficient. For example, Horns Rev offshore wind farm in Denmark is a rectangular grid of 80 2.0 MW turbines spaced at seven rotor diameters (0.56 km). Generating in a wind of 8-10 m/s the yield of the tenth turbine downwind into the grid was reduced to about three-fifths of the output of the most windward machine in the row, suggesting that seven diameters is too close.[5] The power reduction between the windward-most turbine and the next turbine into the grid was "from 100% to 50% between the first two turbines [which] must be considered extremely large".

The conclusion is that repowering on existing wind farm land may be partly counter-productive if the larger turbines wind-shadow each other to a greater extent than happened with smaller machines. US physicist Howard Hayden has pointed out that as machine size and power increase so the necessary spacing increases, both following a square law, thus cancelling the gain.[6] Simplistically, the amount of wind energy which can be collected from a wind farm of given area is constant. Another consequence of power laws is that increasing the diameter of the rotor is initially a very productive way of enhancing wind generation, but it requires more investment in structural materials for tower and rotor. The height-diameter relationship follows a square law but the need for additional strength of materials is cubically related and thus overtakes growth in size and potential generation – this "square-cube" relationship will probably set a maximum size to wind turbines.

The need for balance: spare capacity and spinning reserve

Electricity must be used instantaneously as it is generated. If it is not then the system becomes overloaded, AC frequency and voltage rise, until automatic frequency-sensitive controls ramp-down or trip-out some generating plant. Conversely if demand outstrips generation AC frequency falls, voltage falls and again automatic tripping occurs, this time switching out some consumers, if there is no spare generating capacity available to fill the gap. If these controls are inadequate, cascades of faults may cause failure of parts of, or the entire grid system.

In developed countries the reliability of most generating and electricity delivery systems is very high, so that major failures leading to regional blackout are truly newsworthy events, such as the UK grid-failure of 27 May, 2008. *The Register* wrote of this: "... loss of two big stations so close together caused the frequency of the national grid supply to drop unacceptably as the gap between supply and demand widened. Automatic systems cut in, disconnecting some areas so as to preserve stable supplies for the rest." BBC Radio 4's website responded with the eye-catching headline "Blackout Britain?"

As an insurance against events such as this the National Grid has always attempted to maintain instantly accessible backup power equal to 20 per cent or more of peak demand. Very short term backup demand, up to 2-3 minutes, is met from the inherent inertia of rotating plant and thermal plant boiler steam pressure. From 2-3 minutes to 10-15 minutes can be supplied from ramping the power output of "hot stand-by" spinning reserve, i.e. plant connected to the network busbars but only partly loaded (plus hydro storage and gas turbines). For times over that it takes 8-10 hours to start-up plant from various standby levels.[7]

Because of the short term variability of wind power, when more wind farms are built, maintaining security of supply will become progressively more difficult and steps will have to be taken to ensure adequate backup is available. This is a key problem of wind power and other intermittent renewables and is discussed in detail in the next chapter.

The AC supply system

Discussion of renewable electricity generation often occupies a factual vacuum in which wind turbines seem to be plugged in as easily as attaching a branch to a garden hose. Would that it were so simple!

The electricity supply of all advanced countries is based upon centralised generation of an alternating current (AC) supply, each turbo-alternator in a power station generating at a few thousand

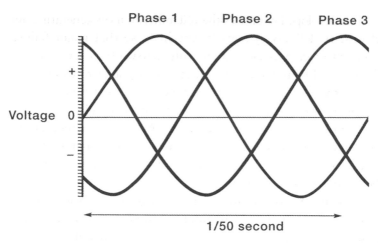

Fig 2.5   Three phase AC voltage/time relationship.

volts(kV) which is then transformed up to the voltage of the national grid – in the UK either 400 kV or 275 kV, as it is more economical to use high voltage for long distance transmission. In the early years of the UK grid, the voltage was 132 kV and in Scotland a part of this 132 kV system is still operated by National Grid and serving under-populated areas, dispersed hydroelectric generators and now wind farms.

Alternating current (AC) is an electric current of which the direction reverses cyclically, as opposed to direct current, whose direction remains constant. The usual waveform of an AC power circuit is a sine wave with a cycle time of 50 per second (50 Hertz) in the UK and tolerance of +1 to -1 per cent (Fig 2.5). The alternators of a grid connected power station are driven at 3,000 rpm, the source of the 50 Hz alternation (3,000/60). The entire UK electricity system is synchronised to the identical 50 Hz AC frequency, a fact of some importance for the connection of small remote wind power generators.

The alternators in a power station are bonded together and their combined output transformed up to the transmission voltage

– in the UK this is the Supergrid 400 kV and 275 kV (plus 132 kV in Scotland). These transmission lines in the UK are operated by the National Grid company and deliver electricity to transformer sub-stations where its voltage is dropped suitably for low voltage distribution. The economy of high voltage transmission is such that an average of only about 1.5% is lost in Supergrid distribution but much greater losses (5%-9% typically) are incurred within the 14 distribution networks feeding homes and industry. AC transmission is used as it makes transforming the voltage upward or downward both simple and efficient. A few high voltage DC long lines are used – including the cross-Channel cables linking the UK to France.

Prior to 1938 there were seven independent grid control areas which supplied Britain but in that year these were joined together to form the National Grid, the largest interconnected electricity system in the world at the time. By reducing the need for independent companies and areas to maintain their own stock of spare generating plant, by 1938 the need for 75% reserve had been reduced to 15%. During The Second World War the ability to transport electricity between regions was crucial to industrial survival and coping with air-raid damage.

The transformer substations on the Supergrid feed 14 distribution networks. These are the penultimate stage before retail delivery and include medium-voltage power lines (mostly 33 kV and 11 kV in the UK), associated transformer equipment and the low voltage delivery lines including 3-phase 415 V and domestic 230 V. The Supergrid operators have no control of events within the distribution networks and see increase and decrease of consumption, or injection of power from "embedded" generation, simply as changes of load at the feeder substations supplying the distribution network. This fact as we shall see has considerable implications for wind power and other relatively small scale renewable generation almost all of which is embedded in the distribution systems.

The problem of linking generators and consumers to the transmission and distribution network is rather more complicated then just closing a switch. The process of connecting an AC generator (alternator) to other alternators is known as synchronisation and is crucial for the generation of AC electrical power, whether it is synchronisation of generators within a power station, or via the extended network of the National Grid.

There are five conditions that must be met before the alternators can be synchronised. The alternator must have equal line voltage, frequency, phase sequence, phase angle and waveform to that of the extended circuit linking all alternators (technically an "infinite busbar"). If any one condition is not met there would be a "spark" on connection – a surge of current which at best would trip-out connected equipment or, at worst, cause such serious overload that damage would be done either to the electrical or mechanical parts of the generating-transmission system.

Most big wind turbines generate AC though at much lower voltage than the grid. They, or control centres in wind farms, need synchronisation before they can feed power to the electricity system. As I wrote above, it is not quite as simple as a new branch on a hosepipe!

References and notes

1. Energy White Paper 2003 *Our energy future – creating a low carbon economy.*
2. DUKES 2008 *Digest of UK Energy Statistics.*
3. DBERR June 2008 (report for) EU 2020 *Renewable Target in the UK Electricity Sector: Renewable Support Schemes.*
4. Sharman H. (2002) Submission to House of Lords Science and Technology Committee. *The Practicalities of Developing Renewable Energy In The UK – In The Light of Danish Experience.*
5. Méchali et al (2006) Wake effects at Horns Rev and their influence on energy production.
   www.dongenergy.com/NR/rdonlyres/575EFE4E-CB73-4D4D-B894-987AC9008027/0/40.pdf
6. Hayden, H. (2004) *The Solar Fraud.*
7. Laughton, M. & P. Spare (2001) "Limits to renewables – how electricity grid issues may constrain the growth of distributed generation" *Energy World*, 01-11-2001.

3 No wind, low wind – intermittent generation

> *"Enthusiasts (and lobbyists enriched by subsidies) who have rushed into extensive wind farm developments will be seen in due course to have taken public opinion for a colossal ride, although this may take some years to emerge."*
> (Lord David Howell and Dr Carol Nakhle: – *Out of the Energy Labyrinth*, 2007)

The first and crucial question is: "What happens when the wind stops blowing?" For a single wind turbine the answer is simply common sense. It stops and no electricity is generated. As we have seen, the wind speed does not even have to drop to zero because generation ceases in the region of 3 to 5 m/s (7 to 11 mph) and furthermore, between this cut-in wind speed and about 15 m/s (34 mph), almost a gale, the machine will be producing less than its maximum output. I shall use the term "intermittent" as a convenient shorthand for this "unpredictably variable and intermittently available generation".

A car's petrol engine will run without its battery – it will survive on the alternator. But stop the engine and it cannot be started again, neither are there any lights if it is dark. The only remedy is outside help. A wind turbine is similarly reliant on an external electricity supply. In the case of network-connected wind farms the lifeline is connection to the AC distribution network. Thus, if a system failure cuts the power supply to a wind farm it will trip-out when synchronicity is lost. It cannot be reconnected to the network until the power supply is reinstated – whether that be correction of a widespread system failure of the grid, repair to a local fault on the distribution network or correction of a problem within the wind farm itself.

Similarly if wind speed falls below the generating level of 3m/s to 5 m/s, as it commonly does, or if it rises to damaging speed above around 25 m/s, or 56 mph, then the wind farm again has to shut down and loses its synchronisation with the network. With modern equipment re-connection may be automatic, as soon as restoration of a live network connection is sensed, or the turbines are able to generate again. As we shall see later, even this automatic capability has been responsible for problems, sometimes on a continent-wide scale.

Individual wind farms, even with sufficient wind, are not of themselves able to restore power to the network after failure because of this problem of matching synchronisation and the other output characteristics. This is often not appreciated but it is a crucial problem of the unpredictably intermittent variability of wind power, and some other renewables such as wave-power. Despite squirming and turning by government, and by the wind industry to conceal the fact, when the "wind engine" stops, there is no recovery without outside help.

Light winds sufficient to depress output to very low levels occur frequently because the cubic relationship of wind speed to energy content dictates that any speed below about 5 m/s gives no significant generation and up to about 10 m/s output is less than 25% of maximum output. Periods of calm weather are not always short-lived. The weather of NW Europe including the UK can be ruled by long periods of high pressure. Older readers will recollect the fabulous summer of 1976 when an anticyclone centred over the Azores lasted for many weeks from about early June – but we did not have wind power then, just a Minister of Drought! As I write at the moment in January 2009, northern Europe and the UK have been effectively becalmed for many days and the real-time wind power records for Germany and Spain have remained between 5% and 10% instantaneous load factor. Unfortunately we have no such real-time monitoring of the UK's wind power but its yield cannot have been significantly greater than of the German wind farms. For a few days a year there is no significant electricity at all from wind turbines throughout Britain, and for much of the year they produce far less than half of their potential maximum. What is more, the output over the whole of the UK is self-correlated – meaning that level of output in say North Wales is often accompanied by similar output in the Highlands and Islands, the North-west and the North-East. It is not possible to present production data for England and Wales as they are not in the public domain. If however we take the Republic of Ireland as a near example it becomes disturbingly obvious that very large areas experience similar wind limitation of generation. Fig 3.1 shows a daily record for the EirGrid wind fleet for the month of March 2008. All other monthly records show similar daily volatility and interspersed long periods of low generation as do similar records for Denmark, Germany, Spain and New South Wales. The claim that the UK is different does not survive examination.

Very often much of NW Europe also experiences the same weather conditions as the UK, a fact which has significance if we consider building a European Supergrid to link and "smooth" wind farm output. A few recent examples are of interest. On the morning of 31 May, 2008 in West Wales I recorded that, "Our Atlantic gale-ridden coast has experienced 2 and 3 mph wind for the last three hours! There are a few 9 and 10 mph readings in E. Anglia and 12 mph at Campbeltown. Stornoway on Lewis 6 mph. So the whole country is effectively in the state of no generation – a shortfall of 2.5 GW." Remember that we need about 10 mph or so for any wind electricity and 34 mph for maximum generation.

Lest readers assume this to be an uncommon event, just a few days later at 1 pm on 2 June, there was not one UK record of a wind speed adequate for any generation except for a couple on the Kent coast (just) – Stornoway, Isle of Lewis 3 mph; Kinloss, Moray Firth 5 mph; Ronaldsway, Isle of Man 6 mph; Culdrose, Cornwall 6 mph; Southend, Essex 3 mph; Kent – Headcorn Aerodrome 3 mph. The two Kent coastal records were Lydd Airport and Langdon Bay 12 mph and 16 mph which would give precious little generation. (Records from http://www.xcweather.co.uk/ and confirmed at http://www.metoffice.com/education/archive/uk/observation_0.htm l).

It is not only simultaneous low wind speeds which cause a problem but also the rapid migration of fronts, usually from the Atlantic, across the UK and into the wind generating areas of Denmark and Germany. Such fronts, with sharp change of wind speed, can cross the UK in just a few hours – a time shorter than needed to bring some thermal generation online (see Chapter 2). Fig 3.1 gives a salutary picture of the rate at which actual wind power output can vary on a regional scale as wind rises and falls. It certainly gives no impression of significant smoothing by the wind "always blowing somewhere".

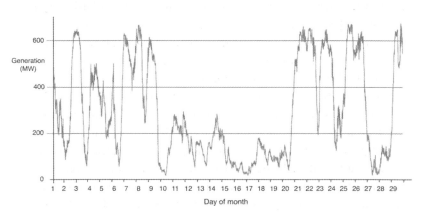

Fig 3.1   Daily output of EirGrid wind power in February 2008. During periods of high wind speed, generation swooped up and down by over 70% of maximum within 24 hours. From days 10 to 20, low wind speed depressed generation to less than 15% of the potential maximum. Source: A. Tubb and Campaign to Limit Onshore Windfarm Development (CLOWD).

There are multiple consequences of wind power intermittency:
1. Generation can be entirely lost and must be replaced by instantly available capacity from another source (usually fossil fuelled generation) which I shall refer to as "backup".

2. Over time, because the generation is often way below maximum, and because wind speed is chaotically variable, the available MW can vary rapidly and unpredictably between zero and maximum and so the fossil fuelled backup must also be able to cope with such fast variation of demand.

3. Over time, fewer than the potential maximum MWh are generated. The ratio between actual MWh generated and the potential maximum is referred to as the Load Factor (see below). The designer of the turbines, the developer and the developers' bankers have a vested interest in predicting this Load Factor as it determines the income and cost-effectiveness of the venture, based on MWh per year generated.

4. If, as politicians often do, it is suggested that wind power may increase security of electricity supply (for example by replacing the need for gas from politically unstable sources) then intermittency affects the "capacity credit" ("firm capacity") of wind power which indicates how much thermal generation could be permanently closed down per unit of wind power installed.

5. Over time, fewer than the potential maximum MWh are generated, thus displacement of fossil fuel carbon dioxide is a function not only of the installed capacity of the turbine(s) but also of the load factor. This is often misunderstood and repeatedly misquoted by the media.

It is not a serious failing in itself that wind power is unpredictably intermittent in yield. Throughout history the corn miller charged sufficient for his flour to compensate for his enforced idleness when the wind did not blow – but the trade became proverbially dishonest. A West Country saying which I learned from the son of a milling family says it all – "You can tell an honest miller by the hairs on the palms of his hands"! Chaucer's miller was the epitome and "could steal corn and full thrice charge his fees".

Wind is not the only natural resource which is intermittent. Rainfall is another and yet all life depends upon it, but water can be stored. Electricity cannot, at least not economically in huge quantities. So – the fact that every kilowatt hour of electricity from these machines must be used instantaneously or spilled – means that the already expensive and low yielding wind turbines have to be shut-down, further reducing their efficacy. The problem is most easily solved if the wind electricity is fed directly into a nationwide grid system in which other flexible sources can be switched-on or off at very short notice. Such sources are conventional fossil-fuelled generators, and using them as backup to balance wind and other renewables imposes limitations and unavoidable expense.

Load Factor and Capacity Credit

Load factor of a wind turbine or other generator indicates the ratio of the electricity it generates during a given period of time, to the energy it would have generated had it run continuously at maximum capacity for that period (usually a specified year). In the US "capacity factor" is used synonymously and also in the UK by the BWEA for reasons best known to itself.

Because there are so many days of overall low electricity yield, the average load factor of wind farms in the UK is low. DBERR's recent figures (Table 3.1) show that onshore turbines have averaged only 26% during the past 5 years and surprisingly, offshore wind farms have performed no better.[1]

The low load factor does not matter *per se* as it is allowed for in financial projections and with huge hidden subsidies (Chapter 4) a 25% load factor can still be profitable. What is much more important for the integration of wind power is that there is no way of knowing whether there will be electricity tomorrow morning – or even this evening. Of course this is why those pre-Second World War aerogenerators in the US were sold as a package with "batteries included". However, at present there is no economically viable way of storing electricity in quantities sufficient to smooth industrial wind power through periods of low generation, and

Table 3.1 Annual wind-generated GWh for 2007, percentage of electricity supply and load factors (data from DUKES, 2008, Table 7.4)

Wind Power	GWh/y	Load factor	% total supply	Average 5 year load factor (4 offshore)
Onshore	4,491	27.5%	1.1	26.4%
Offshore	783	25.6%	0.2	26.4%
Total	5,274	26.6%	1.3	26%

% total electricity supply based on 3401,671 GWh (DUKES 2008 Table 5.5)

probably never will be. For that reason wind stations must be coupled to the conventional electricity system which provides the necessary backup of reserve generating capacity. Such backup is akin to insurance – a protection against accidental and unpredictable failures.

Capacity Credit is the statistical capability of wind energy to replace conventional power plant and is also known as "firm capacity"; "secured capacity" or "secured total output". It is defined as the percentage of conventional power plant which could be shut-down and replaced by wind power, without making the system significantly less reliable. If all wind turbines continuously generated at maximum output, the capacity credit would be 100% but this is never achieved in practice, as most of the time wind turbines will be well below maximum output. If wind power is to be considered as direct replacement for the megawattage of fossil fuelled power, capacity credit is of great importance and it is no surprise to find that argument has raged over its level. In 2005 the CEO of E.ON Netz claimed that wind capacity credit in Germany was about 8% and was likely to fall to 4% if the 2020 target could be achieved.[2] E.ON Netz is the operator of one of the largest assemblages of wind turbines in the world and might be expected to know its business. This order of magnitude was also suggested by the DENA Report[3] which assessed the present day capacity credit of wind power in Germany as 6% of installed wind capacity. More recently E.ON UK said that:

> It could take 50 gigawatts of renewable electricity generation to meet the EU target. But it would require up to 90% of this amount as backup from coal and gas plants to ensure supply when intermittent renewable supplies were not available. That would push Britain's installed thermal power base from the existing 76 gigawatts to 120 gigawatts. (*The Guardian*, 4 June, 2008)

Electricity supply with high capacity credit is described as "despatchable" – in other words available at any time to satisfy demand (or capable of being ramped down to balance a fall in demand). In response to a Parliamentary question asking what contribution is provided by "plant development under the renewables obligation in providing despatchable capacity . . ." the Secretary of State for BERR, Malcolm Wicks replied "2,046 MW" but specifically excluded "wind and solar" generation, thus acknowledging both sources as non-despatchable.[4] Effectively this implies that they are of zero or very low capacity credit and reinforces the statement:

> Wind power is really not "dispatchable" – you can't necessarily start it up when you most need it. (University of Massachusetts Renewable Energy factsheet)

In this context alone any attempt to claim wind power as contributing security of supply must be not only flawed but dishonest. For example the DBERR's *Wind Power: 10 Myths Explained* includes the following implying high capacity credit:

> The geographical spread of wind farms minimises the loss of generation when the wind stops in any one location . . .

Flawed and dishonest it may be, but several counter claims must be examined, particularly the vehement denial in a recent report, commissioned by the DTI from the Oxford Environmental Change Institute[5] purporting to demolish the argument for a backup requirement by claiming that the wind always blows somewhere in the UK. This resulted in Energy Minister, Malcolm Wicks, claiming:

> This new research is a nail in the coffin of some of the exaggerated myths peddled by opponents of wind power. (*The Independent*, 14 November, 2005)

However the Oxford report simply compared the incidence of wind speed permitting "no generation" with a wind speed allowing "some generation", however little. Had it compared incidence of generation above a sensible threshold (say 20%) with incidence of maximum generation it would have been apparent that in anticyclonic weather there are many occasions per year when the whole UK wind fleet would be contributing very little. This was indeed realised by the House of Lords Science and Technology Committee in February 2004 when Baroness Platt of Writtle questioned Mr Sinden, the lead author of the report. He replied:

> The analysis that I ran was of wind speeds being so low that electricity would not be generated . . . If you raise the bar higher and say "We want 20 per cent output or 30 per cent output" then it may look a little bit different but we have not carried out that analysis.

The UK National Grid's Seven Year Statement (SYS) claims that:

> For 25,000MW of wind, only 5,000MW of conventional capacity can be decommissioned.[6]

However this estimate of 20% capacity credit is so much higher than for example the E.ON Netz 4% to 8% cited above that one must question it. The original suggestion can be traced back to a paper by Dale, Milborrow, Stark & Strbac in *Power UK*, Issue 109, March, 2003, which said that:

> for a small level of wind penetration the capacity value of wind is roughly equal to its load factor, approximately 35%. But as the capacity of wind generation increases, the marginal contribution declines. For the level of wind penetration of 26 GW, about 5 GW of conventional capacity could be displaced, giving a capacity credit of about 20%.

The huge overestimation of load factor – 35% versus the realised 26% is hardly conducive to trust.

An earlier National Grid SYS 2003 however wrote:

> In any event, should more response and reserve services be required, then our ancillary service market arrangements should encourage their cost effective provision.

It should not escape us that the National Grid does not itself have to provide the reserve generation and is free to make such a suggestion irrespective of costs and practicability. The corresponding section of the current SYS 2008 adds:

> . . . the wind capacity that can be taken as firm is not proportional to the expected wind energy production. It follows that the electricity market will need to maintain in service a larger proportion of conventional generation capacity despite reduced load factors. Such plant is often referred to as "standby plant" . . .

Backup (Standby or Reserve Capacity)

The foregoing discussion shows that the unpredictability of wind demands the constant availability of conventional generating capacity to provide extra electricity or to balance over-production because electricity has to be consumed instantaneously as it is generated, or generated to satisfy instantaneous demand.

This is acknowledged by the BWEA's Frequently Asked Questions Page which says:

> When the wind stops blowing, electricity continues to be provided by other forms of generation, such as gas or coal-fired power plants . . .

As we shall see there is dissent about the amount of generation that can be provided from intermittent renewables without incurring the need for dedicated backup. Whether it is 5%, or 10% of total generation is arguable but if the spare capacity which insures against major plant or transmission failure is locked-up by a sudden change of wind speed then the insurance is no longer available. Elsewhere I have likened this to lending your neighbour half your property insurance – at no extra cost – try it and see what the insurance company says! If one could flick a switch and have instant access to a "cold" power station the problem would be solved but this is not so. None of our nuclear Magnox and AGR stations can be switched on or off quickly, and a coal fired power station takes many hours to come in from the cold, Combined cycle gas turbine stations (CCGTs) are faster but not designed for constant throttling up and down whilst a small amount of open circuit gas turbine generation (OCGT) is instantly accessible but very expensive and carbon-profligate.

A recent report by the UK Energy Research Centre (UKERC)[7] was aimed at dispelling claims that intermittency is a problem. Despite this, the report admits that:

> Wind generation does mean that the output of fossil fuel-plant needs to be adjusted more frequently, to cope with fluctuations in output. Some power stations will be operated below their maximum output to facilitate this,

and extra system balancing reserves will be needed.
Efficiency may be reduced as a result.

This last point is an admission that more fossil fuel will be burned
to support the variable behaviour of wind power.

The Department of Trade and Industry (now DBERR) must
have been warned some years ago that intermittency would require
provision of dedicated backup. In a 2003 documentary for BBC2,
Dr Dieter Helm, Energy Economist and Fellow in Economics, New
College, Oxford, said of wind power:

> What we know, is the wind blows sufficient for these
> windmills to be producing about 35%, perhaps 40% of the
> time. So the paradox of building windmills is that you have
> to build a lot of ordinary power stations to back them up
> and those are going to be almost certainly gas in the short
> to medium term and that's what's required. If you ask the
> question who's making sure that there's enough gas stations
> out there to back up the windmills the answer is nobody.
> (BBC2 programme *If . . . The Lights Go Out*, 2003)

Dr Helm had been on the DTI Energy Advisory Panel since 1993.
In passing, I think even the industry would now agree Dr Helm's
upper limit of 40% for load factor was over-optimistic. Practical
experience and the Renewables Obligation Certificate (ROC)
Registers now suggest an onshore average of about 28%. Also the
expression of load factor as a "per cent of time" is not strictly
correct but a common misconstruction.

The most recent and positive statement that there is a
problem is in a report to the Scottish Executive (2006)[8] which,
among other conclusions, said:

> there will be many hours in a year when renewable output
> from wind, waves and tidal currents falls below demand
> targets and balancing plant would be needed.

Reading the above account no one could be blamed for concluding that this was one of those childhood exchanges – "tis . . . tisn't . . . tis . . . tisn't . . ." and so on forever. That this is happening and that the British Wind Energy Association and UK government are devoting so much effort to disproving the obvious, seems evidence enough to me. The reports from E.ON Netz and E.ON UK were written by working wind power engineers and all imply that intermittency is a serious problem on the Atlantic seaboard and further away in Germany on the fringes of continental Europe. It will be a problem here in the UK, whatever the DBERR wishes us to believe. I discount the Oxford report[5] which accidentally (or deliberately) used a zero generation as a baseline and thus concluded that there would always be "some" generation. So what if a few turbines on an outer Scottish island may be lazily turning with the rest of the country becalmed? There is a case to be answered as suggested by ABS Energy Research in 2006.[9]

> Be wary when the wind industry describes a criticism of wind power as a "myth". Industry figures like the Chief Executive Officers of E.ON Netz and Eltra do not deal in myths and solutions, they have real experience and more data than anyone else. They record what has actually happened.

Several of the reports I have quoted also suggest there is no real problem up to the 2010 target of 10% of electricity from all renewables – of which 75% to 80% will have to be wind. The reason given is that there is already back-up in place.

BWEA's FAQ for example claims:

> When the wind stops blowing, electricity continues to be provided by other forms of generation, such as gas etc. Our electricity system is mostly made up of large power stations, and the system has to be able to cope if one of these large plants goes out of action. It is possible to have up to 10%

of the country's needs met by intermittent energy sources such as wind energy, without having to make any significant changes to the way the system operates.

The UKERC 2006 report[7] similarly says:

> There may already be more than sufficient reserve capacity on the system to deal with intermittency – particularly if the amount of intermittent generation is a small proportion of total supply.

It is quite correct that reserve capacity is provided for the conventional generating system. The National Grid plc aims for a system margin of about 20% over peak demand thus insuring against generating plant or transmission failure. Some of this spare capacity would be on "hot standby", i.e. connected to the network and operating at part load to ensure a stability of connection as in the case of steam plant, or available for instant start-up and connection as is the case for hydro and gas-turbine plant.

It is this instant start-up component which wind power calls upon to smooth its short term vagaries and it is dishonest of the wind power industry and BERR to claim:

> The reserves needed to guard against loss of a large power station will readily cope with the small perturbations due to the wind.

This may be true at the moment, with wind power providing less than one per cent of average generation from an installed capacity of just over 2000 MW but if the contribution of wind power should rise to (say) 10% of average generation i.e. 4,500 MW we would need a wind installed capacity of up to 18,000 MW to provide it at a load factor of 25%. Thus within a period of just a few hours, wind output could swing by a substantial fraction of 18,000 MW, balanced against that peak load insurance of 20% (which represents about 11,000 MW). It can't be done and if we build the governments "heroic" target of 33 GW offshore plus some 17 GW onshore, is patently ludicrous. We shall in due course need a bigger insurance policy and as Dr Helm said, and must have said to the DTI, "the paradox of building windmills is that you have to build a lot of ordinary power stations to back them up . . ."

The real world

The problem of inadequate reserve generation has already arisen in other countries. On 1 March, 2005 the Spanish grid operator, Red Electrica Española, advised 300 heavy electricity users it was going to avail itself of the interruption clause in their contract. Then, their electricity supply was cut off. The reason for this was made clear by Radio España's Radio Litoral news bulletin which explained the "brownout", saying the wind had dropped and reduced the electricity production of 11,000 windmills to 700 MW. Spain was unprecedentedly cold at the time, demand for electricity was high, gas reserves were low, and 5,000 MW of reserve capacity were out of commission and so the loss of wind power created a risk of blackout. Hence the decision to pre-empt this by reducing demand in a controlled sector. It is not fortuitous that almost 6.9 GW of new gas-fired CCGT plant has been installed in Spain since 2002, and a further 6.8 GW is under construction!

In February 2008 Texas experienced an exactly similar "system event" as a result of too little wind power and too little spare capacity. The wind-feed from west Texas fell rapidly from 1,700 MW to 300 MW out of a total installed wind capacity of about 4,000 MW. The Electric Reliability Council of Texas explained that this coincided with increasing evening electric demand as temperatures fell. System operators cut power to interruptible customers to reduce demand by 1,100 MW within 10 minutes.

"Interruptible" customers may become less happy about their reduced tariffs if cuts with ten minutes warning become much more frequent. This Texas event was caused by a shortfall of about 1,400

MW out of a running total demand of 35,000 MW at the time. Even today in the UK, we could easily experience dropout of 2,000 MW from wind when total demand is say 50,000 MW. In both cases this is about 4% – so are we already vulnerable?

It is not only the triggering of failure by wind power which is a threat. The volatility which wind, other renewables and localised heat and power (CHP) impose, out of instrumental view by transmission system operators (TSOs), can cause serious problems. On 4 November, 2006 Europe's largest ever power failure blacked out 15 million consumers connected to the Union for the Co-ordination of Transmission of Energy (UCTE) European grid which sprawls between Portugal and the Balkans.

The first problem was a cascade failure triggered by the routine switching out of a power line crossing the Ems river to allow passage of a vessel. UCTE's 2007 report[10] concluded that wind power, though not the cause, was a substantial factor increasing the scale of failure and inhibiting recovery.

About 40% of the total generated power which tripped during the incident was wind power units and 60% of the wind generation connected to the grid tripped just after the frequency drop caused by the incident. Similarly, 30% of combined-heat-and-power units in operation just before the event, tripped during the frequency drop. Significantly only one high power thermal generation unit of about 700 MW tripped (in Spain). Consequent on these events the European grid split into three areas no longer synchronised nor connected:

> Recovering the frequency to its nominal value required an increase of generation output in the Western area and a decrease of generation output in the North-Eastern area. After a few minutes, wind farms were automatically reconnected to the grid, being out of the TSOs' control. This unexpected reconnection had a very negative impact, preventing the dispatchers in both areas from managing the situation.

The report concluded:

> The negative role of wind generation performance on 4
> November was evident. Due to uncontrolled behaviour of
> wind generation it was not possible to maintain a sufficient
> power exchange balance in some German control areas . . .
> after split.

We could not have a better example of the threat we face. Had the
TSOs not had access to instantly available hydro-electricity and
remote generating reserves the event would not have been
controlled so quickly. The situation is indeed worse in the UK,
because we are islanded and have only the 2 GW cross-Channel
link to France and even now are not capable of supplying or
carrying our maximum wind output, despite only 1.3% of supply
coming from wind and peak wind generation being no more than
about 4% of average total generation.

Shortly after reporting on this Europe-wide power failure
UCTE published its study on integrating wind power into
electricity grids.[11] Some of its main findings were that:

> The increasing share of wind power and the regional
> concentration in certain areas might lead to grid situations
> with sudden capacity losses of more than 3,000 MW which
> could be followed by large-scale blackouts.

And to provide security against this eventuality:

> The variable contributions from wind power must be
> balanced almost completely with other back-up generation
> capacity located elsewhere . . . Furthermore, a considerable
> amount of reserve capacity – being paid [for] by the
> consumers – is needed for system adequacy and security.

Another salutary warning was that:

High wind power production remote from main electricity demand centres produces higher grid losses within the transmission system.

This gives the lie to vociferous claims that localised wind power (or other renewable) will reduce such losses. This could only be done if we envisage individual homes providing their own "green" power, which we have already seen might involve a 20-fold redundancy of generating equipment – a ludicrous concept when related to an already expensive technology.

The findings of the 2008 House of Lords Select Committee on The Economics of Renewable Energy[12] make it eminently clear that this will be the case:

> To make up for its intermittency . . . back-up conventional plant will be essential to guarantee supply when required, to compensate for wind's very low capacity credit. Wind generation should be viewed largely as additional capacity to that which will need to be provided, in any event, by more reliable means; and the evidence suggests that its full costs, although declining over time, remain significantly higher than those of conventional or nuclear generation.

This is not by any means a new observation:

> Regardless of the amount of wind power capacity installed, wind generation has no reserve-capacity credit. It follows that the entire peak load plus reserve margin has to be covered by conventional plant as at present.[13]

It is my view that the BWEA and the DBERR are misleading us over this matter. There is certainly no consensus that intermittent wind power can be fed into our electricity network in large quantities without action being taken soon, to ensure stability and security of supply. The government and wind industries wish us to believe that 10% of generation can be reached with no problem. My opinion is that difficulty will be encountered at well below this target and that the saving of CO_2 emission will be so small as to be unjustifiable, as discussed in Chapter 5. Almost all evidence to the contrary has been produced not by the power industry itself but by individuals or organisations commissioned by the vested interests of wind power.

DBERR's "myths" statement that emissions savings lost through use of fossil fuel back-up will be minimal to 2010 is either an admission that wind power, by 2010 will be but a tiny proportion of total generation, or it implies that we are not being told the truth about the real impact and cost-benefit of wind power. If the ludicrous suggestions for a total of 50 GW from wind including 33 GW offshore are implemented we shall run full tilt into the paradox of needing nearly as much extra conventional capacity as of wind – as E.ON UK said.

Notes and references

1. DBERR (2008) Digest of UK Energy Statistics (DUKES).
2. E.ON Netz (2005). Press release from CEO Martin Fuchs, accompanying *Wind Power Report 2005*.
3. DENA (2005) Planning of the Grid Integration of Wind Energy in Germany Onshore and Offshore up to the Year 2020. Deutsche Energie-Agentur GmbH (German Energy Agency)
4. *Hansard* (9 Jan, 2008) : Column 677W.
5. Oxford Environmental Change Institute (2005) *Windpower and the UK Wind Resource*, ed Graham Sinden.
6. National Grid SYS 2008 (Seven Year Statement 2008).
7. UKERC (2006) *The Costs and Impacts of Intermittency* (UK Energy Research Centre)
8. University of Edinburgh (2006) *Matching Renewable Electricity Generation with Demand*. Commissioned by the Scottish Executive.
9. ABS Energy Research (2006) ABS Windpower Report.
10. UCTE (2007a) Final Report – *System Disturbance On 4 November, 2006*.
11. UCTE (2007b) Towards a Successful Integration of Wind Power into European Electricity Grids.
12. House of Lords Select Committee (Economic Affairs) 4th Report of Session 2007–08 *The Economics of Renewable Energy*.
13. Laughton, M (2002) *Platts Power In Europe*.

4 Financing the impossible

He was a jester and could poetize, But mostly all of sin and ribaldries. He could steal corn and full thrice charge his fees; And yet he had a thumb of gold, begad. (Chaucer, *Canterbury Tales.* "The Miller's portrait")

During the twenty-first century, renewably generated electricity in the UK, largely wind power, has earned its generator and/or supplier up to three times as much per MWh as thermal generation. The consumer does not know this as the extra cost has been paid as a hidden subsidy. This is financed by increases in electricity bills but has never been explicitly stated or explained. Even now, with the high wholesale electricity prices during 2008, the covert subsidy pays the industry an additional three-quarters of the real value of the electricity.

There is probably no country in the world where grid connected wind power is deployed without its receiving a very large subsidy in some form or other, usually paid by all electricity consumers or by all taxpayers and often both. These payments are obfuscated by complex and deliberately concealed mechanisms, and often directly misrepresented by government. The Welsh Assembly for example is on record as saying under the headline "Myths and Legends":

There are no direct subsidies for wind farms.[1]

Further misinformation is propagated by the enormous range of green tariffs for retail electricity, all of which create the impression that the subscriber is cutting carbon dioxide (CO_2) emission thereby saving the planet. The raw truth is that the ordinary UK consumers – who far outnumber green tariff subscribers – are paying by far the largest proportion of the exorbitant subsidy to wind power. Government itself has admitted[2] that this subsidy (which it denies elsewhere!) "will provide support of £1 billion per year by 2010 to the renewable industry".

The reason for this huge consumer-sourced subsidy is that wind power, though it is the cheapest of the newer renewables, is still remarkably expensive considering that the energy source is free. In November 2008, the UK Minister for Energy and Climate Change told Parliament that gas fired and coal fired electricity costs just over £50 per MWh to generate. Offshore wind power is almost twice this at £92/MWh with onshore wind at £72/MWh.[3] Comparison with nuclear generation shows an even greater gap, the Minister's estimate being £38/MWh. As a matter of interest, in France, with a very large proportion of nuclear power (almost 80%), cost of generation is near £30/MWh (early 2009).

These figures are the basic cost of generation. Wholesale electricity comprising the grid-mix of fossil fuelled and nuclear sourced power was marketing at median price of £60-£70/MWh on a typical day of the week during which the Minister made the above statement of costs. Such is the volatility in the half hour bidding periods that this average included a low of below £40/MWh and a peak above £160/MWh. These wholesale prices are what the generator would be paid by the National Grid or other purchasing body before payment of additional premiums on renewables. Retail sale to domestic consumers is at a much higher rate of about £145/MWh (14.50p/kWh) or night time (Economy 7) discounted electricity at £78/MWh, both with the addition of an account standing charge.

Wind power is remarkably expensive in capital investment for a given output. Onshore wind turbines cost up to about £1.25 million to build, per MW of installed capacity, and with a load factor of 30% this represents £4.2 million capital per average achieved MW power output. Offshore wind is almost twice this –

perhaps £7 million to £8 million capital per average achieved MW. Compare this with AREVA's new nuclear European Pressurised Reactor (EPR) under construction at Flamanville in France. This will cost about £1m to £2m per achieved MW, assuming baseload operation with a 90% load factor and will have low future fuel costs (compared with fossil fuelled power). Furthermore Ofgem has recently expressed the view that investment of £20 billion, equal to the National Grid's present capital value, will be necessary to reinforce transmission to cope with the dispersed and remote nature of wind power and other intermittents (*Sunday Times*, 3 August, 2008).

As we saw in Chapter 3, the output of a fleet of wind turbines, spread over a substantial area of a country such as the UK, or even the entirety of northern Europe, shows considerable self correlation – indicating that they are all experiencing similar wind weather. Thus the unpredictable intermittency of output we have already seen is a characteristic of whole countries as well as individual machines. Statistically the implication is that only a small proportion of the total wind generation can be relied on to be available at any one time, perhaps falling to no more than 4% of installed capacity.[4] By contrast, the output from any new fossil fuelled power station, or from a nuclear station such as the Finnish EPR, would be of great reliability with a capacity credit well above 90% and operable at 80% to 90% load factor compared with the weather-constrained 25% to 30% load factor of wind farms.

So there we have the problem. Would you continue to visit a shop which was often and unpredictably closed and when open could rarely supply you with a desired commodity and at twice the supermarket price? Of course not, and the only way such an establishment could avoid bankruptcy would be legislation to keep it open and a constant drip-feed of cash from another source to cover the losses incurred by the constant closures and repeated failures to supply goods, despite high cost.

This is precisely what has been done world wide for the wind power "shop". In the UK we have legislation which creates an obligation to purchase the electricity whenever available and however poor the quality of supply. Similar legislation has allowed the growth of Denmark's and Germany's large wind industries and in the US a system of covert tax-breaks and offsets serves the same purpose.

The UK Renewables Obligation (RO) and Climate Change Levy exemption (CCLe)

Two financial measures in the UK are intended to promote the development of renewable electricity generation. The RO is effectively a consumer-sourced subsidy whilst the CCLe is a tax-break, protecting a renewable power generator from paying an energy tax.

The Renewables Obligation (RO) was introduced on 1 April, 2002 replacing the former NFFO (Non-fossil Fuel Obligation). A series of RO Orders dating from 2002 were made under the Electricity Act 1989, obliging suppliers to purchase set percentages of electricity from renewable generators (wind, biomass combustion etc). In 2002/2003 the requirement was 3% from "renewable, rising through 9.1% in 2008/2009, and reaching 15.4% in 2015/2016". For historical reasons hydro-electricity from large scale generators (above 20 MW) is not eligible for RO or CCLe as it is already considered a mature technology, not in need of subsidy. The UK Government announced in the 2006 Energy Review an additional target of 20% by 2020-21 and made a pre-budget announcement in 2008 that the RO was guaranteed until 2037.

In principle the RO is simple, requiring the supplier to purchase the specified percentage and punishing failure with a fine. The provision of the necessary renewable electricity to the supplier is acknowledged by the issue of Renewables Obligation Certificates (ROCs) from the Office of Gas and Electricity Markets (Ofgem), one ROC being issued for each eligible megawatt hour of renewable energy generated. ROCs have a pre-set financial value but may also be traded, and thus acquire an additional commodity value.

The Climate Change Levy (CCL) is a tax on energy delivered to non-domestic users, introduced on 1 April, 2001 under the Finance Act 2000. However, renewable electricity suppliers are not required to pay this tax – hence the CCL exemption, and their electricity is consequently more valuable to them than conventional thermal generation. Despite emitting no carbon dioxide, nuclear power is not eligible for ROCs neither does it receive the CCLe. Until 2007, each MWh of renewable electricity effectively received £4.30 by not having to pay the CCL and from 2007 this sum has been index linked (£4.56 in 2008). With wholesale electricity currently in the region of £60-£70/MWh the CCLe is a relatively small reward.

Unlike the CCLe it cannot be said that the ROC income is small! When the RO was introduced in 2002, the basic buy-out value of the ROC was set at £30/MWh, index linked, and today (2008) has risen to £35.76. Because the certificates were permitted to be a marketable commodity and are in demand by suppliers which have not bought sufficient renewable power, the value may be inflated to near twice the buy-out value (up to £55/MWh in late 2008). The combination of ROC buy-out and market value represented a huge premium in the early years of the RO. For example in 2002 wholesale electricity was less than £20/MWh so the combination of ROC buy-out and market value more than trebled its worth. Even now when wholesale electricity has risen to £60-70/MWh a subsidy of over £50/MWh is a huge level of support, unprecedented in other industries and likely to grow again as a proportion of value now oil and the linked gas prices have dropped so dramatically to less than a third of mid-2008 levels.

If this explanation is difficult to understand it was meant to be! The flow chart of Fig 4.1 may clarify the issue. The electricity output is reported to Ofgem by the generator [1] which receives equivalent ROCs [2]. Those ROCs can be sold with the electricity to a supplier [3] or the certificates can be sold in the marketplace [4]. Suppliers who have bought insufficient renewable electricity can purchase ROCs in the market [5] to avoid being fined. The

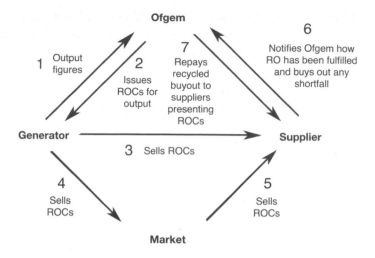

Fig 4.1   The Renewables Obligation Cycle. One Renewables Obligation Certificate (ROC) is awarded by Ofgem for each MWh of electricity exported by an accredited Generator. The Generator can sell the ROCs together with the electricity to a Supplier, or as a separate commodity. Suppliers present ROCs to Ofgem and/or pay the buy-out price to comply with their Renewables Obligation to buy a set percentage of renewable electricity (3% in 2002-3 rising to 10.4% in 2010). Ofgem pools the buy-out as a "ROCpot" which is redistributed to suppliers in proportion to their ROCs presented/ Total ROCs. Ofgem terms this "recycled buyout" (or the market significantly calls it "the green smear").

supplier can then notify Ofgem of the renewable electricity bought with ROCs in evidence and pay for any shortfall at the buy-out price – effectively a fine [6]. Ofgem pools the buy-out income and returns it to suppliers in proportion to the renewable electricity they have provided [7]. It is this possibility of the buy-out reward which drives the market value of a ROC above its basic buy-out value.

Thus renewable energy is financed by the threefold mechanism of the Renewables Obligation (RO), the Climate Change Levy exemption (CCLe) and the marketing of RO Certificates (ROCs), the complexity of which is difficult for the public and the media to unravel. This obscurity seems a quite deliberate attempt to conceal the fact that the RO and CCLe are effectively a hidden tax on all electricity consumers and a huge hidden subsidy to providers of renewable energy – larger indeed than any subsidy in history.

In summary the mechanisms and their value are, for 2008:

1. The Renewables Obligation buyout price – £35.76/MWh.
2. A trading increment from marketing of Renewables Obligation Certificates – currently near £20/MWh.
3. The Climate Change Levy exemption – £4.56/MWh.

These three thus total £35.76 + c. £20 + £4.56 = approximately £60 per MWh, which is added to the wholesale value of the electricity generated by wind power.

If the wind power generator and supplier are one and the same firm (e.g. npower) the net result in the first year or two of the RO was that wind electricity created an income for the generator approaching three times that paid for thermal generation. Even now, in late 2008, this about doubles the value of wind -electricity and other eligible renewables. An effective subsidy to three times unit-cost is gigantic, historically unprecedented and I believe unsustainable. Coal-firing currently receives less than one twenty-fifth of this subsidy whilst gas and nuclear generation get none at all (former DTI personal-communication). If the generator and supplier are separate companies the subsidy is shared between them.

This is a huge premium on wind power and its crucial importance may be gauged from the statement by Paul Golby, the chief executive of E-ON UK (former Powergen), who said:

"Without the renewable obligation certificates nobody would be building wind farms." (*Daily Telegraph*, 26 March, 2005).

When the RO was first introduced in 2002 I described it as the product of "brilliant spin doctoring" because no one would ever understand how it worked! This is manifestly true as, seven years later, the media have generally failed to appreciated the fact that the RO is not just a requirement to purchase but is tied-in to a consumer sourced subsidy of gigantic proportion. This failure allows the industry and politicians to claim that wind power is not directly subsidised with relatively little fear of challenge in the media.

Where does the money come from?

DTI's 2003 Energy White Paper said:

> We have . . . introduced a Renewables Obligation for England and Wales in April 2002. This will incentivise generators to supply progressively higher levels of renewable energy over time. The cost is met through higher prices to consumers.

The other, smaller premium, the CCLe is paid for by all taxpayers and again I quote the 2003 White Paper:

> By 2010, it is estimated that this support [RO] and Climate Change Levy (CCL) exemption will be worth around £1 billion a year to the UK renewables industry.

Thus ALL consumers pay the cost, not just those who get a warm glow by switching to a "green" tariff to receive exactly the same electricity via their sockets! Indeed these "green" consumers pay much less in total toward renewables because there are far fewer of them than the 20 million or more ordinary customers. In a recent leaflet explaining electricity bills, Ofgem has pointed out that even now, with only a tiny proportion of renewable electricity:

> The Renewables Obligation . . . adds around £10 to an electricity bill per year and is set to rise to around £20 per year by 2015.

The leaflet also lists other associated on-costs including the EU Emissions Trading Scheme, the CERT (Carbon Emissions Reduction Target) and reinforcement of Transmission network.

These are estimated respectively at an additional £31; £38 (combined electricity and gas deduction) and £1.37 p.a. by 2008 – in all, over £80 added to fuel-poverty.

The burden on consumers is set to increase as the White Paper of 2007 (Meeting the Energy Challenge) contained proposals for banding the RO to provide different levels of payment for different renewables. In the context of this chapter offshore wind power is set to receive 1.5 ROCs per MWh as opposed to one ROC at the moment.

The House of Commons Committee of Public Accounts reported on the RO in 2005, commenting that:

> Despite the reference to consumers' interests in the wording of the Government's 2010 target, however, the Department [DTI] has not consulted consumers, or their representative groups, about their willingness to contribute to the cost of renewable energy.

and also said:

> There is no annual parliamentary approval of the cost to consumers of supporting the renewables industry through the Renewables Obligation . . . [because] Parliament does not consider the subsidy to the renewable industry as part of the annual supply procedure.

One might as well say the suppliers have been given *carte blanche* to charge the consumer whatever they wish to finance this dubiously useful scheme.

Renewable support in other countries

Three main types of reward for renewable power may be offered: these are green certificates, tax incentives and feed-in tariffs. In Europe, the UK's RO is an example of green certification, which is also the mechanism in Sweden, Italy, Belgium and Poland. In all these cases the certificates are in themselves tradable commodities. The UK's additional and smaller CCLe arrangement is a tax incentive and is used in Malta and Finland as the sole support of renewable generation but generally in most countries is an additional policy tool as it is in the UK (e.g. Cyprus and the Czech Republic).

Feed-in tariffs encourage the generation of renewable energy by obliging electricity suppliers to purchase renewably generated electricity at a premium above market rates, usually over a guaranteed time period. They are described as "feed-in" laws as they encourage renewable generators, including small generators, to feed excess electricity into the grid. Feed-in tariffs are particularly aimed to encourage small and medium sized generators and may be a fixed rate of payment or a premium rate payment in which government sets a fixed premium or an environmental bonus, paid above the normal or spot electricity price.

In France, with a feed-in tariff arrangement the organisation Vent du Boccage has written:

> French conventional electricity (nuclear, thermal and hydro-) is less than 0,030 Euro per kWh. The electricity from windmills is purchase by EDF (national electricity corporation), at 0,0832 Euro per kWh (2 to 3 times normal price of electricity) a price guaranteed by the French government for a long period (10 to 15 years).

Three countries in Europe have a particularly large take-up of wind power: Denmark, Germany and Spain. In 2002 Denmark replaced its earlier wind power subsidy with a premium feed-in tariff for onshore and a tendering system for offshore wind farms. Prices are valid for 10 years. The tariff subsidies roughly compensate the very heavy taxation of household power in Denmark. Interestingly the pre-2003 subsidies were much higher and since their replacement by the reduced tariff of DKK 0.60/kWh (about 7p/kWh), new onshore wind turbine installation has virtually come to a standstill.

In Germany, feed-in tariffs are guaranteed for 20 years – about 11-14 Eurocents per kWh in 2008 (up to £114/MWh). There is also an option for tax incentives in addition. In Spain there is choice between a fixed feed-in tariff or a premium on top of the conventional electricity price. Both cover the entire lifetime of the wind farm and pay up to 107.97 Euros per MWh (£102/MWh). The additional, per MWh, payments are of a similar order in all countries and must in every case represent unprecedented levels of subsidy on the entire product of a single industry.

Outside Europe we find a very similar situation with huge and concealed benefits to the wind power developers and covert arrangements which prevent this from being common knowledge. Australia's MRET (Mandatory Renewable Energy Target) law for example gives emphasis to large projects using tradable certificates legislation and is one of the first such legally enforceable schemes in the world.

The situation in the US is probably the most complex of all with some six mechanisms which are exploited to reward the wind power developer at the expense of consumers and tax-payers. They are: 1. Federal Production Tax Credit for wind power; 2. Accelerated Depreciation – allows substantial deduction from taxable income; 3. Avoidance of State Corporate Taxes; 4. State production tax credits or subsidies for Wind Farm owners; 5. State Renewable Portfolio Standard (RPS); 6. Other Tax Breaks and Subsidies.

Most of these arrangements have a self-evident function in rewarding the wind power generator but the RPS needs explanation. Effectively it is a State legal requirement that a growing percentage of the electricity sold in their state must come from renewables (mostly wind). So lucrative is the US arrangement that UK-based BP and Netherlands-based Shell are investing heavily in wind power in the US. This gives good green street-cred but also permits the two companies "to avoid tens or hundreds of millions in federal and state income tax on their profits, including oil profits".[5] It is a matter of interest that both of these multinationals have withdrawn from the UK wind power market which, despite its huge subsidies, is less profitable than the US.

Capital subsidy

The repeated claim that "There are no direct subsidies for wind farms" is deliberately misleading – a smoke and mirrors matter when we consider that the accumulated RO and CCLe subsidy income alone, during a projected life of about 25 years, will be more than £3.5 million per installed megawatt. It is also a specifically untrue claim for offshore wind farms which have been and are in receipt of large sums of government sourced subsidy as well as money from other sources such as lottery funds. For example in 2006 the Secretary of State for Trade and Industry told Parliament that in the period 2004-2006, £34.7 million of direct capital subsidy was paid to six offshore wind farms.[6] In the same year the Permanent Secretary to the Department of Culture, Media and Sport wrote in response to an enquiry:

> I understand that Burbo Bank received £10 million funding under the Big Lottery Fund's £50 million programme for renewable energy projects throughout the UK, which is dedicated to building offshore wind projects. Signed Dame Sue Street, 3 April, 2006.

The future deployment of gigantic offshore wind farms will presumably absorb capital subsidy in like fashion – one cannot otherwise see how the industry could be persuaded to take on the huge extra expense and risk.

References and notes

1. National Assembly for Wales (2003) *Renewable Energy Report*.
2 This statement appeared in the Energy White Paper 2003, and was reiterated in 2005 by the then Secretary of State for Trade and Industry, (*Hansard*, 14 Nov, 2005 : Column 888W).
3. *Hansard*, 11 Nov, 2008: Column 1133W.
4. E.ON Netz (2005). Press release from CEO Martin Fuchs, accompanying *Wind Power Report 2005*.
5. Schleede, 2008, pers. comm.
6. *Hansard*, 23 Jan, 2006: Column 1770W.

5   Do wind turbines abate carbon emission?

Harnessing the natural power of the wind is essential to tackle global warming. (Yes2wind website)

The current "Dash for Wind" could actually make the situation worse. (UK Power, 2004)

A great many words have been devoted to the question of how much carbon dioxide (CO_2) emission wind turbines mitigate or even whether they pay back the energy which is used in their building. "Myths" abound on both sides of the debate!

Before diving into this murky pool, consider the situation for fossil-fuelled or nuclear power generation. It is inconceivable that a modern civilisation could function without electricity. The energy which is used in the construction of conventional power stations comes mainly in the form of heat from fuel combustion, and it is irrelevant whether the subsequent electricity output pays back this energy during the life of the plant. We would build the power stations even if the energy balance were seriously negative. Just for the record, it isn't – the payback time is 2 or 3 years for conventional power stations.[1] It is also the case that there was very strong opposition to the building of many of our conventional power stations. I witnessed this as a young man and it has taken half a lifetime to realise that if we all want our comfortable, medically cared for, lives then these 1950s and '60s stations had to be steam-rollered into place in an act of foresight. This argument in no way applies to wind power and the recently proposed overthrow of planning law to facilitate deployment of wind turbines is an outrage against common sense. The generating yield is so unstable compared with thermal generation that it can never provide either baseload or load-following electricity and there will always be need for thermal plant with installed capacity equal at least to peak demand plus an insurance reserve of say 20% (see Chapter 4).

The unpredictability of wind power dictates that the power could not be sold in the marketplace unless legislation forces the issue. Thus irrespective of energy payback, and despite wind power having existed as a fairly mature technology since the 1930s, it came to nothing as no one could sell wobbly wind electricity in competition with reliable mains-connected power.

This remained the case until the 1970s-80s when along came the suspicion that man-made CO_2 accumulating in the atmosphere might cause climatic warming. For the wind power developer this was the quack-doctor's dream – a putative "illness" for which snake-oil was an obviously logical cure. Wind turbines emit no CO_2 but make perfect and very expensive medicine for climate change.

To assess whether this proposed remedy for climate change has any real effect we need to examine two things. Firstly, do the machines actually make a positive contribution; that is do they pay-off the energy and carbon cost of construction? Secondly, if and when construction carbon has been paid-off, can wind power provide enough carbon-free electricity to make a worth-while difference?

A wind turbine needs no fuel and it produces electricity which undisputedly can displace power which would otherwise come from fossil fuel. Simplistically we could assume that a megawatt hour (MWh) of renewable electricity from the wind displaces a MWh of thermal generation. This is precisely what BERR implies in its *Wind Power: 10 Myths Explained* statement:

> Every unit of energy generated by wind doesn't need to be generated by carbon-producing sources.[2]

Let's have a look at this assumption and try to quantify it. One megawatt installed capacity of wind power generates an average 0.3 MW assuming a generous load factor of 30%. The annual electricity yield would thus be 0.3 x 365 x 24 = 2,628 MWh/y and multiplying this by the CO_2-cost of generating 1.0 MWh will give the emission saving if the one to one displacement is correct.

It is not simple to allocate a CO_2 conversion factor as different thermal generators produce differing amounts of CO_2 and as older inefficient power stations have been replaced the factor has diminished with time. At the present coal is the dirtiest, emitting 0.86 t CO_2/MWh, gas fired generation produces 0.36 t CO_2/MWh and nuclear virtually no CO_2 emission (data from power station annual Environmental Performance Reviews). The average mixture of generating fuels results in a present day "grid-mix" of 0.43 t CO_2/MWh.[3] These MWh figures are equivalent to 860 g CO_2/kWh, 360 g CO_2/kWh and 430 g CO_2/kWh.

From the early years of wind power in the UK, the BWEA has maintained that all wind-generated electricity displaces coal-fired generation and the Association's calculation page said that:

> BWEA calculations use typical emissions from coal-fired plant of 860g CO_2/kWh.

Thus the 1.0 MW of installed capacity would save 2,260 tonnes CO_2 per year (2628 MWh x 0.86 t CO_2/MWh). This claim has been repeatedly challenged, in particular by complaints to the Advertising Standards Authority (ASA) which almost routinely failed until 2007 when a complaint concerning npower's use of the 860 g factor at Batsworthy Cross wind farm (Devon) was upheld.

BWEA was forced to issue the following statement in a press release of 15 October, 2007:

> The ASA found that BWEA member company npower had breached its rules by using a figure of 860 g/kWh for CO_2 displacement for its proposed new Batsworthy Cross

wind farm and the BWEA Chief Executive announced that "The industry has been pro-actively working with the ASA since the Summer to agree a robust and verifiable set of figures, as well as an agreed methodology so that the new figures can be regularly updated in future."[4]

More than a year later no further agreement had been publicised but the Association's calculation page[5] was amended during 2008 to read:

> BWEA calculations use a static figure representing the energy mix in the UK: 430g CO_2/kWh.

This may all seem to be an esoteric argument about a few numbers, but the significance is that at a click of a keyboard the wind industry has been forced to agree that it will need twice as many wind turbines to achieve a set carbon target and because the costs of wind generation closely reflect capital expenditure the cost of saving each tonne of CO_2 emission with wind power will be doubled.

This U-turn by the BWEA may not be the end of the matter as the figure of 430g CO_2/kWh implies that the grid-mix is displaced. As gas-fired generation of electricity grows and coal is phased-out it will become increasingly likely that the lower CO_2 emission of gas firing will be displaced by wind electricity. The report from the Sustainable Development Commission (SDC), Windpower in the UK[6] also suggests this lower CO_2 displacement:

> There are large differences between the CO_2 emissions associated with coal (243 t C/GWh) compared to natural gas (97 t C/GWh), with none associated to nuclear power [and continues]: for the purpose of this report, it has been assumed that wind output will displace the average emissions resulting from gas fired plant... it is the figure that the DTI use and is used here so that the carbon benefits of wind power are not overestimated.

[note that these two CO_2-equivalence factors are expressed as tonnes of carbon per GWh which convert to 890 g CO_2 /kWh and 360 g CO_2 /kWh].

Thus the present situation (late 2008) is that displacement of 860 g CO_2 /kWh (coal) is discredited. The BWEA now claims 430 g CO_2 /kWh (grid-mix) and if gas fired generation continues to expand, the factor will fall toward 360 g CO_2 /kWh (or even less if nuclear percentage increases with load following PWR technology). In 1990 gas comprised 0.5% of all UK generation, by 2007 it had increased to 43% and is still rising fast. Nuclear has fallen from 21% in 2000 to 15% in 2007 with further closures predicted but government now intends to reverse this.

Calculated on current generating-mix, each MW of installed wind power capacity, at a generous 30% load factor, displaces no more than 1,130 tonne CO_2 (2,628 MWh x 0.43 t/MWh) per year. The BWEA claimed in late 2008 that the UK had an installed capacity of 3,174 MW which, at the same generous 30%, would annually mitigate 3,586,746 tonne CO_2. However as of December 2008 the BWEA was still claiming twice this: 7,174,545 though by late January 2009 a new data-base page gave the more reasonable halved figure.

An additional exaggeration relates to the claimed installed capacity and load factor. The DBERR figure for installed wind power capacity in 2007 was 2,477 MW with an actual generation of 5,274 GWh[7] representing 2,267,820 tonne CO_2 for the year 2007 using the 430 t CO_2 /GWh factor). This is less than one third of BWEA's original claim which even allowing an extra years growth in capacity is a huge overestimate of reality. If it was an intentional misrepresentation it is an offence to use false information in a planning application. Such permissions may well be void if a legal challenge could be mounted.

The wind power industry has claimed that a wind turbine pays back the energy consumption of its construction (and the consequent CO_2 emission) within a few months[8] and DBERR's *Wind Power: 10 Myths Explained* currently claims:

> The average UK wind farm will pay back the energy used
> in its manufacture within three to five months.[2]

Given the dissimulation about CO_2 and energy equivalence it is reasonably to suspect that "three to five" months is also a dubious claim. The House of Lords must have thought so when its Science and Technology Committee[1] claimed a 1.1 year energy payback.

Use of energy and emission of CO_2 in construction and deployment of wind turbines is not the only source which must be balanced against the promised saving of emission by the machines. All soils contain a substantial quantity of organic material and in the case of very wet and acid soils this may be a layer of almost pure organic peat cover, which in extreme conditions may be many metres deep. The wetness prevents atmospheric oxygen from entering the peat and, coupled with the acidity, greatly reduces the rate of bacterial breakdown and CO_2 release which limits the organic content of drier soils.

If a wind farm is built on deep peat, site operations such as excavation for foundations and road construction cause drying and there may be substantial CO_2 emission from its oxidation *in situ* or after water or wind erosion. This has been specifically observed by the Environmental Management Committee at Cefn Croes (mid-Wales) which wrote:

> ... oxidation of exposed peat was leading to a huge loss of
> carbon to the atmosphere, and mitigating the impacts of
> the Wind Farm from a Global Warming perspective.

Recent attempts to quantify this additional CO_2 loss suggest that the period of about one year for balancing the engineering CO_2 cost may be substantially extended. A study by M. J. Hall[9] suggests that a wind farm on a one metre depth of blanket peat might have a CO_2 payback time of 3.6 years of which turbine construction and installation comprise 1.1 years. This must be kept in proportion, as a relatively small proportion of wind farms are on such deep peat deposits.

The cash cost of a wind turbine is a very different matter from the energy budget, as a large proportion of the cost derives from value-additive operations such as the complex engineering of the drive train and generator and the specialist fabrication of blades which are skilled labour intensive but do not consume much energy. The main energy cost and CO_2 emission is in the smelting of iron and its conversion to steel and to a lesser extent, manufacture of other metals. Arguably, without enormous subsidy, a wind turbine could not pay back its financial cost in a reasonable time-frame (see Chapter 4).

How much CO_2 from backup?

We saw in Chapter 3 that it is impossible for substantial wind power to be absorbed by the electricity transmission and distribution system without dedicated provision of backup generation from thermal stations – as the BWEA's website says:

> More [than 10%] can be accommodated, but extra storage capacity or spinning reserve would be necessary . . .

It is difficult to calculate the amount of CO_2 which is liberated from power stations providing back-up for renewable electricity generation but this amount must be subtracted from the theoretical saving of CO_2 emission. Wind power is supported by thermal generation which is operating below peak generation and can be ramped up to cover losses of generation when the wind stops blowing. This causes fuel inefficiency and emission of extra CO_2 per unit of electricity generated by the backup.

At present, as we have seen, the backup is taken from the existing reserve capacity used as insurance against plant and transmission failure. The wind power industry, unfairly, has argued that because the backup is pre-existing, there are no CO_2 costs.

Be that as it may, it is not a situation which will persist. Once the demands of wind power for cover for its full installed capacity are sufficient to call upon a large proportion of existing reserve it will be necessary to build dedicated backup. It is this requirement that prompted the Irish National Grid to conclude that:

> As wind contribution increases, the effectiveness of adding additional wind to reduce emissions diminishes…The cost will be very substantial because of the backup need.[10]

At least some power engineers have attempted to calculate CO_2 costs in these circumstances, thus Bass & Wilmott (2004) claimed, for a worst-case scenario, that their analysis

> suggests that the current "Dash for Wind" could actually make the situation worse.[11]

The degree to which control of CO_2 emission is compromised is still a matter of argument. West Denmark, with the highest *per capita* proportion of wind power generation in the world has also been warned:

> Increased development of wind turbines does not reduce Danish CO_2 emissions [beyond the present capacity].[12]

It is certainly the case that Danish *per capita* CO_2 emission is one of the highest in Europe and that most of the country's consumption is sourced from fossil fuelled generation, imported hydro-electric and imported nuclear power whilst a large proportion of its purportedly record-breaking wind power is perforce exported at peppercorn prices.

The assumption that one MWh of wind generation displaces one MWh of thermal generation is falsified by the acknowledged need for backup from-ready-to-generate plant. Sir Donald Miller, former Chair of Scottish Power, told the Whinash public inquiry[13] that this would impose a 20% or greater loss of the CO_2 advantage as fuel use is inefficient when backup plant is run below peak load as is necessary to provide instant access. This argument already applies to the reserve generation which our small wind fleet uses as backup, effectively "stolen" from the backup power intended to secure conventional supply. When wind power increases substantially, dedicated conventional plant will be necessary to ride through periods of low wind speed. E.ON UK has estimated a need to increase Britain's installed power base from the existing 76 gigawatts to 120 GW to accommodate the vagary of the proposed 50 GW of installed wind capacity.

There is a further concealed penalty of providing backup "insurance" as it will only be used infrequently though some must be kept hot and ready to generate all the time. This will dramatically increase the CO_2 payback time of such plant – normally about 2 years[1] – as well as making it uneconomic. The spectre arises that yet another subsidy will be needed to get backup generators built in the first place. A similar argument applies to the additional transmission capacity which has to be built. This needs the capacity to carry 3 to 4 times the average wind power output (25% to 30% load factor) to cope with high wind – exacerbated by the fact that most large scale wind power will be built in remote areas or offshore. The National Grid has admitted that thus upgrading needs an investment equal to the current capital value of the system!

Is the saving worthwhile?

The Intergovernmental Panel on Climate Change's Fourth Assessment Report (2007) says quite unequivocally:

> Both past and future anthropogenic carbon dioxide emissions will continue to contribute to warming and sea level rise for more than a millennium.

At the time this prompted a vivid mental image of William the Conqueror battling toward the South Downs intending to alter the environment of Britain in 2066. Joking aside there is a fairly low limit to the amount of wind power which can be deployed without the need for backup becoming counterproductive.

Because of this, the Government's own figure for saving of CO_2 emission by renewable power generation, mainly wind, is just 9.2 million tonnes per year by 2010 (quoted by the Department for Environment, Food and Rural Affairs (DEFRA) and DBERR as 2.5 Mt carbon). This is less than the emission from a medium sized coal fired power station and more to the point is less than four ten-thousandths (0.0004) of global total CO_2 emission and stands no chance of altering atmospheric CO_2 concentration, still less deflecting climate change over a millennial period!

References and notes

1. House of Lords (2004) 4th Report of Session 2003-04 *Renewable Energy: Practicalities*. Appendix 8.
2. DBERR web-page *Wind Power: 10 Myths Explained*.
3. DEFRA web-page Fuel Conversion Factors.
    http://www.defra.gov.uk/environment/business/envrp/gas/05.htm
4. BWEA press release ("Wind industry to agree new CO_2 reduction figures with Advertising Standards Authority." Tuesday, 15 October, 2007).
5. BWEA amended calculations web page.
    http://www.bwea.com/edu/calcs.html
6. Sustainable Development Commission (2005). *Windpower in the UK*. See p35 of corrected version dated November, 2005 (units were incorrect in 1st edn).
7. DUKES (2008) Digest of UK Energy Statistics.
8. Danish Wind Turbine Manufacturing Organisation (1997). *The Energy Balance of Modern Wind Turbines*. Wind Power 16 (Krohn, S. ed).
9. Hall, M. J (2006) Peat, Carbon Dioxide Payback and Wind Farms. Renewable Energy Foundation (REF)
10. Irish National Grid, Electricity Supply Board (ESB) (2004). *Impact of Wind Power Generation in Ireland on the Operation of Conventional Plant and the Economic Implications*.
11. Bass, R.J. & Wilmot, P (2004) Wind Power may not be the answer. *UK Power Issue 2*.
12. ELSAM (2004) Presentation by Flemming Nissen, Head of Development, Elsam A/S to a conference on wind power in the future energy system, held at the Dansk Design Centre.
13. Sir Donald Miller (2005) Evidence to the Public Inquiry, proposed Whinash wind farm, Cumbria.

6   Landscape degradation and wildlife

The Government's thesis that the countryside of upland and coastal Britain is "worth sacrificing to save the planet" is an insult to science, economics and politics. But the greatest insult is to aesthetics. The trouble is that aesthetics has no way of answering back. (Simon Jenkins, *The Times*, 24 October, 2003)

Wind turbines are natural elements in the landscape. (Danish Wind Industry Association website)

Every twist and turn of Britain's lanes and byways opens a new heart-stopping vista. Each hedge and hillside hides changes of geology and geography in a patchwork map of incredible beauty. Much of this diversity is a living history of our country, with its wild upland spaces, field patterns, villages and farmsteads, the whole rimmed around by a coast which is largely unspoiled despite our tiny land area and relatively huge population. Yes it is nearly all man-made – but by man the craftsman, man the unconscious artist, whose efforts created John O'Gaunt's "precious stone set in the silver sea" – a treasure which only a philistine or a traitor would seek to destroy.

But this indeed is what the wind power industry is bent on doing – to drive roadway after roadway through lonely places, to dump concrete in enormous quantity, to bulldoze acres of hillside into wind farms studded with gigantic, identically mass-produced steel and plastic monsters. This is akin to demolishing the great cathedrals for road stone or shredding the contents of the National Gallery to make wall insulation. What hatred of national identity could envisage such a body blow? One is reminded of Defence Secretary Rumsfeld's remark on the stripping of Iraq's archaeological treasures: "Things happen." They do indeed, and often with the connivance of the powerful!

Simon Jenkins' eloquent railing against the wind industry which heads this chapter is indeed well founded – an insult to science and economics at an aesthetic cost which is unacceptable. We have seen in previous chapters that it is difficult to justify wind power in terms of cost-benefit, even before we consider its destructive impact on landscape. The saving of carbon dioxide emission, the original justification, is never honestly factored in, and the industry is judged politically solely by its achievement of targets, which are set in the deceptive terms of installed megawatts capacity or "homes supported".

The industry and its political supporters have spread a pernicious smokescreen of propaganda. BWEA calls wind turbines "A valuable addition to the landscape"; DBERR claims:

> In most cases, people found that their worries about landscape impacts and noise were unfounded, with surprising numbers even finding the wind farms a positive addition;

and Yes2wind tells us:

> While some people express concern about the effect wind turbines have on the beauty of our landscape, others see them as elegant and beautiful.

Yes2wind is incidentally a consortium including WWF, FoE and Greenpeace. If these machines are so elegant, so beautiful an addition to the countryside, why does the Scottish Executive's Planning Policy 6 (PP6) planning advice say that:

> . . . development up to 2 km is likely to be a prominent feature in an open landscape. The Scottish Ministers would support this as a separation. [to define broad areas of search].

Why for that matter, if wind turbines are "elegant" supplements to landscape, should a Public Inquiry Inspector have written the following in dismissing an appeal by Enertrag against a decision of Broadland District Council (Norfolk)?

> Overall, I consider this area is not one that can accommodate a group of six very large structures without serious visual harm. The intimate nature of the small-scale agricultural landscape would be severely disrupted visually by the introduction of man-made structures of the size proposed. The height of the towers and blades, and the movement of the latter, would compete visually with some listed buildings, notably the churches . . . which form such key points of reference in the gently undulating landform.

This balanced assessment concerned a site with no special landscape designation but close to an Area of Important Landscape Quality.[1]

Yes2wind goes further down the route that landscape is not worth preserving as:

> Climate change will severely and irrevocably alter much of our landscape as well as the animal and plant life.

Invocation of the wind power-CO_2-landscape argument is perhaps the most extreme of untruths for we have already seen that wind power could not significantly alter CO_2 concentration and in any case even cessation of CO_2 emission sufficient to totally stabilise atmospheric CO_2-content would, by IPCC's own admission, not stop man-made climate change as it:

> . . . will continue to contribute to warming and sea level rise for more than a millennium.[2]

Repetition becomes truth? Windmills will alter the weather and save us all. Unless of course one looks at the repeated huge majority objections to wind power schemes. For example the Scottish Executive received 11,397 objections to the revised application for the Lewis Wind Farm in the north west of the island, with only 59 letters in support of the scheme (*Stornoway Gazette* 29 March, 2007)! At the opposite end of the British Isles, Yelland Wind Farm (Devon) received 1,496 letters of objection to the proposal and six in favour submitted to a Public Inquiry (June 2006). There are many more examples.

Precisely the same majority against wind is now found by most on-line or telephone polls (for what they are worth, being so open to fiddling). The *Western Mail* asked "Would you be happy to live near a wind farm?" The result was yes, 14% and no, 86%!! (5 December, 2008). The *South Wales Evening Post* asked a similar question on Nov 27, 2008 and recorded 29% for wind power and 71% against. It is of interest that these two papers cover an area of much natural beauty, with few wind farms but with an imminent threat of large-scale development including Gamesa's proposal for 600 foot turbines! How, one asks, does BWEA repeatedly find so different a story? It reports that the DTI commissioned GfK NOP Social Research to conduct a survey which showed "81% are in favour of wind power" and a survey conducted by Mori for EDF Energy showed "72% of people supported wind farms . . ." A stark and suspicious contrast with the answer, "No, 86%".

Where is land targeted? The map of wind speed distribution in the UK is very similar to a topographic map of the country. Wind speed is greater in upland than lowland areas with the exception of higher speed "rim" around sections of the coast.[3] The Danish Wind Industry Association's website says it all when it proclaims:

> Look for a view . . . we would like to have as wide and open
> a view as possible in the prevailing wind direction.

Enertrag, in a recent Public Inquiry concerning 125 m turbines, admitted that there would be significant visual impact up to a distance of 10 km, in other words over 300 square kilometres. A view indeed! It is worse than simple visibility from a distance – with blades rotating, flickering reflected light, projecting shadows or silhouetted against the sky, wind turbines are much, much more visually intrusive than a static object of the same size, not that there are many 300 to 400 foot static structures in the countryside.

Man, crops and stock thrive better when sheltered, so these coasts and uplands are often our last remaining wilderness areas of semi-natural land: Britain's "green-lungs" and havens of peace for the mending of broken souls. Of course it is no coincidence that our Designated Areas – National Parks, Areas of Outstanding Natural Beauty and many Sites of Special Scientific Interest etc – are mostly within these precious pre-industrial landscape remnants. Yes – the landscapes are largely man-made, from the prehistoric past, which is why we call them "semi-natural" but at the present time they are the only parts of our tiny country where one can be free of an obvious human footprint for the precious leisure hours. They also provide the habitat for much of our rarer flora and fauna which are allowed to flourish by the solitude.

Thus, the wind power developers generally covet the most beautiful areas with the highest wind speed which give the greatest output and the highest return. However, because of the original NFFO subsidy and the subsequent covert subsidy of the RO, most of the UK is at risk. The quest for "a view" has led to the uplands and coast being exploited first and it has even been suggested that such places have deliberately been the first targeted – with the rationale that a despoiled landscape can no longer be advanced as an argument for protection.

This pursuit of hilltop and coastal locations was the inspiration of Cameron McNeish's moving lament over the most remote Scottish Corbett, Carn na Saobhaidhe:

> I wept tears of frustration at man's arrogance and greed. I wept tears of helplessness that people like me, to whom these wild places mean everything, couldn't effectively fight the political/corporate forces that are determined to

steal Scotland's soul in the name of green energy. And I wept tears of genuine sorrow that my children's children wouldn't enjoy these places as I have done.[4]

Oh, Cameron, not in Scotland alone are tears of frustration shed. A green countenance never was so sick a colour of cynicism.

The undoubted and unavoidable impact on landscape beauty has often been a key factor in withholding of planning permission, or the failure of planning appeals by developers. The three national planning advice documents for England (PPS 22), Scotland (NPPG 6 & SPP 6) and Wales (TAN 8) give some small measure of protection against wind power development in designated areas. These include National Scenic Areas, Sites of Special Scientific Interest [SSSI], National Nature Reserves (NNR), National Parks and Natural Heritage Areas, Areas of Outstanding Natural Beauty (AONB), Heritage Coasts, Scheduled Monuments, Conservation Areas, Listed Buildings, Registered Historic Battlefields and Registered Parks and Gardens as well as international natural heritage designations such as Ramsar sites, Special Protection Areas [SPAs] and Special Areas of Conservation [SACs].

The control is not entire – for example NPPG 6 says:

> . . . renewable energy projects, which would have an adverse effect on the conservation interests for which the site has been designated, should only be permitted where there is no alternative solution and there are imperative reasons of over-riding public interest." More worryingly PPS 22 includes "Small-scale developments should be permitted within areas such as National Parks, Areas of Outstanding Natural Beauty and Heritage Coasts provided that there is no significant environmental detriment to the area concerned.

The area of designated land is considerable: some 3.5 million hectares of land, freshwater and coastal seas, representing 10 per cent of the UK land area (http://www.jncc.gov.uk/page-4241).

I opened with Simon Jenkins "aesthetics has no way of answering back". Just occasionally it has, for example a Public Inquiry Inspector, rejecting a development appeal in Berkshire, said that it "would be prominent and intrusive and have a significant and adverse effect on the qualities of the landscape thus failing to conserve and enhance the natural beauty of the North Wessex Downs Area of Outstanding Natural Beauty".[5] Unfortunately we do not all have the fortune to live in or near designated landscapes and it is no surprise that developers frequently say this in planning applications. The perception that some landscapes are up for grabs is further promoted by the ill-conceived remark from campaigners that "We are not against wind power *per se*" – an unconscious bit of nimbyism which is in fact a kick in the teeth for many like-minded souls. It is just a thoughtless act like throwing litter out of a car – forgetting that others reap the benefit but may be a false move, for as we have seen there are better arguments than landscape, against the building of network-connected wind farms.

The "build it over there" attitude may also rebound in the long term as more than 90 per cent of rural dwellers live outside designated areas which may be someone else's "over there". Nowhere is this more cynically obvious than in Wales' TAN 8 planning advice which proposes that the majority of wind power development shall be confined to Strategic Search Areas (SSA) of low population density and lacking landscape or wildlife designation. Not only is this unfair to the residents of the SSAs, it projects a false image of landscape value as the quality of habitat and aesthetic appeal in the SSAs is often equal to that of designated areas – it is just a fortuity that, for example, the Cambrian Mountains never became the National Park which was once proposed.

The constraint of the SSAs is furthermore not quite what it seems. The wording is that "large scale (over 25 MW) onshore wind developments should be concentrated into particular areas . . . " (the SSAs). At the time this was written there were no wind farms bigger than 25 MW in Wales! This proviso of course will permit applications of less than 25 MW anywhere in the country – and will inevitably happen. The pressure to open land to subsidised wind power is immense and will if unchecked engulf the whole UK now that planning protection is so reduced in power, whilst the myth grows that windmills will somehow change the weather.

Wildlife – birds

By far the strongest reaction to wind power development and wildlife has been driven by reports from various parts of the world that birds and bats are killed by rotor blades. This is hardly surprising. Wind turbines are so gigantic that, though the rotor appears to be travelling quite slowly, the blade tip velocity of a big machine often exceeds 150 mph – two or three times the motorway speed limit. Anyone who has struck a bird with a car will know that even a 20 mph collision is lethal. A bird which just avoids a blade tip has just over a second to dodge the next blade, approaching from about 80 to 90 yards away on a curved path and probably outside the range at which many birds would perceive a moving hazard, even in good visibility. For example a V80 machine gives about 77 yards sightline and 1.2 seconds until the next blade arrives – this might exercise a fighter pilot's skill!

It did not take the developers long to realise that the reported death of golden eagles and other raptors, for example totalling 1,700 annually at California's enormous Altamont Pass wind "factory", was a potential publicity disaster. This was later compounded by reports of bats dying in large numbers at wind farms worldwide, as most bat species are threatened.

Quickly, the dismissive responses appeared: "Quite simply, birds are in far more danger from colliding with overhead power lines, or being eaten by domestic cats, or hit by vehicles than they are from wind turbines . . ." (BWEA website). Who last saw a domestic pussy-cat wrestling a golden eagle to the ground for the *coup de grace*? DBERR's "Myths" website is even more devious on the matter: "A paper in *Nature*, by a large group of scientists including one from the Royal Society for the Protection of Birds (RSPB), indicated that in sample regions covering about 20% of the Earth's land surface – 15% to 37% of species (not just birds) will be committed to extinction as a result of mid-range climate warming scenarios by 2050." A half truth concealing a lie, as we have seen that wind energy is unlikely to make even a marginal difference to the CO_2 emissions being blamed for climate warming.

The RSPB has not helped public understanding as it has repeatedly made the point that it supports development of wind power because it helps mitigate climate change which "poses the most significant long-term threat to the environment..." (Yes2wind). Again there is little truth that wind power will influence man-made climate change even if it is happening, which is widely and increasingly disputed. Even if we fully accepted the "warming" scenario, the IPCC's 2007 report concluded that even if we stabilise atmospheric CO_2:

> Both past and future anthropogenic carbon dioxide emissions will continue to contribute to warming and sea level rise for more than a millennium.[2]

However, despite the RSPB's support for wind power, the organisation has more recently acknowledged that birds may suffer. An objection was lodged to Amec/British Energy's 600 MW scheme for the Isle of Lewis: "We believe this wind farm proposal is not just bad for birds but bad for the development of renewables as well, as the area is protected under European law for a variety of important birds, including golden eagles, merlins, black-throated divers, red-throated divers, dunlins and greenshanks." This development has now been refused permission but not all RSPB objections are effective. At Edinbane on Skye planning consent was granted despite RSPB's contention that the site was too close to sea eagles and several breeding pairs of golden eagles, as well as merlin and hen harriers. An RSPB officer commented anonymously: "The fact is we don't really know what will happen. Developers do environmental assessments but they own the research. And consultants are under pressure from the energy companies for the right answers." (*Observer*, 5 October, 2003). Some developers do not dispute the risk, for example at nPower's proposed Mynydd-y-Gwair and the nearby Mynydd Betws developments the Environmental Impact Assessment (EIA) admits that "cumulative impacts on red kite [will] be significant at geographical scales in excess of 'local', should both wind farms be constructed". Table 6.1 perhaps shows the problem more than mere words.

These reports highlight the main fear that the very large, slow flying raptors are most at risk and in the UK these are mostly rare and potentially threatened species. Many hunt for food on the ground beneath by "telescoping" from above and may have no self-protective instinct against attack from the air (what attacks an eagle in flight?). The fact that kite and vulture have proved the most likely raptors to die in European wind farms supports this interpretation as they circle, searching for food below, and may not even take great notice of the hurtling blades. Two red kite deaths have already been confirmed in mid-Wales where there are only a relatively small number of turbines as yet.

The Brandenburg figures in the table relied on scoring corpses found by the public. Many will be missed, and scavengers such as fox and badger may remove many more. Direct studies intended to detect bird death reveal disturbing numbers in habitats similar to many in the UK. At three wind farms in Flanders (Belgium) the collision numbers varied from 0 to 125 birds per wind turbine per year. The mean number in 2002 was 24, 35 and 18 birds per wind turbine per year at the three farms.[6]

In the US:

Table 6.1 Records of raptor deaths at wind farms

Species killed	Number recorded	Location	Source
Red kite	99	Germany since 2001	1.
Buzzard	95	do.	1.
White-tailed sea eagles	32	do.	1.
White-tailed sea eagles and golden eagle	12	Gotland, Sweden	2.
White-tailed sea eagles	4	Smola, Norway 5 months	3.
Raptors including golden eagle	Up to 1,300 per year	Altamont Pass Ca over 25 years	4.
All birds	Up to 4,700 per year	do.	4.

1. Brandenburg State Environment Office central record of bird deaths. http://www.mluv.brandenburg.de/cms/media.php/2334/wka_vogel.pdf Source: Tobias Dürr Landesumweltamt Brandenburg 2008.
2. Ornithological Society of Gotland 2008.
3. Alv Ottar Folkestad, Norwegian Ornithological Society 2005.
4. http://baynature.org/articles/jan-mar-2009/altamont-power-struggle

Research by raptor experts for the California Energy Commission (CEC) indicates that each year, Altamont Pass wind turbines kill an estimated 881 to 1,300 birds of prey, including more than 75 golden eagles, several hundred red-tailed hawks, several hundred burrowing owls, and hundreds of additional raptors including American kestrels, great horned owls, ferruginous hawks, and barn owls. These kills of over 40 different bird species violate federal and state wildlife protection laws.

(http://www.biologicaldiversity.org/swcbd/programs/bdes/al
tamont/altamont.html)

Smallwood and Thelander (2004) reported to the CEC:

> The assertion that [Altamont Pass] is anomalous in its bird
> mortality is largely untrue . . . Whereas the available
> data suggest that [Altamont] kills more raptors than
> do other wind energy generating facilities, the risk index
> demonstrates that [Altamont] kills no more raptors relative
> to the number seen per hour than do most other wind
> energy facilities. Adjusting for local relative abundance,
> the existing data indicate that most wind energy generating
> facilities have an equal impact on the local raptors.[7]

In September 2005, the *San Francisco Chronicle* reported that half
of the 5,000 windmills in the Altamont Pass will be closed for three
months this winter to protect migratory birds following years of
protests from environmentalists. However the Altamont Pass
Avian Monitoring Team reported in early 2008 that "annual
fatalities do not appear to be decreasing despite the . . . winter
shutdown program, high risk turbine removal and blade-painting."

If Smallwood and Thelander are correct about correction for
abundance, once some of the big wind stations are built we are
likely to see unacceptable losses of rare raptors. Scottish National
Heritage (SNH) has recently written to the Scottish Executive
admitting that collision risk to sea eagles and golden eagles at the
proposed Muaitheabhal Windfarm had been underestimated by a
factor of about 54 times (Letter dated 5 December, 2005). This
alters a predicted kill of one golden eagle every 3 to 6 years to an
outrageous, one per 3 to 6 weeks. SNH repeated in this letter that
it was willing to continue to discuss, with the developer, any means
of achieving an "acceptable collision risk".

Despite such evidence, the wind power developers and RSPB
in the UK have dismissed the huge toll of raptors at Altamont Pass,

saying it is on a migration route and irrelevant to the UK. In a legal information leaflet the RSPB cites the law concerning birds, that it is "an offence to use traps or similar items to kill, injure or take wild birds". Of course there are "exception" clauses but given the minimal advantage of building wind farms, should there be? It is also a salutary exercise to read RSPB's strident support for wind power in its short report RSPB ADVOCACY (2008) on promotion of biodiversity in which the words "wind power", "wind turbine" or "wind energy" occur some 20 times but the word "electricity" just once – and then tied to "nuclear"! How many RSPB members are aware that the society says of the Thames Array proposal that it "protects sensitive wildlife interests, whilst allowing an important renewable energy development to proceed"?

Wildlife – bats

It was not until early 2004 that news really spread about the vulnerability of bats to wind turbines. Wendy Williams, a journalist for *Windpower Monthly* published "When Blade Meets Bat" in *Scientific American* (Feb. 2004) and recorded the death of at least 400 migrating bats at Mountaineer Wind Energy Centre, Backbone Mountain, West Virginia. Other publications suggest that allowing for carcasses missed, or carried off by scavengers, over 2,000 bats were killed and possibly many more at this site.

Bats navigate by echo location but cannot cope with the speed of wind turbine blades and are most vulnerable when the wind speed is low, which is when their prey is flying and bat activity is greatest. There is also suspicion that bats may actually be attracted to the neighbourhood of turbines. A recent paper suggested that bats actively forage near operating turbines: rather than simply passing through turbine sites, they approached both rotating and stationary blades and followed or were trapped in blade-tip vortices. They also investigated the various parts of the turbine with repeated fly-bys, and were struck directly by rotating blades.[8]

It is apparent that some bats die of shock and are found dead but uninjured beneath the machines, probably from being buffeted by wake vortices. Recently, autopsies on such casualties have revealed tissue damage to the lungs which is consistent with the sudden pressure changes which will occur if the animal is trapped in a trailing vortex.[9] The injury is comparable with barotrauma suffered by SCUBA divers when descending or ascending too quickly.

It is of interest that UK law makes it an offence knowingly to "Set and use articles capable of catching, injuring or killing a bat . . ." or to "Possess articles capable of being used to commit an offence, or to attempt to commit an offence." (Bat Conservation Trust information leaflet). Natural England has acknowledged that a problem may arise. Its "Bats and onshore wind turbines: Interim guidance" however suggests:

> The information currently available about the behaviour of bats in the UK is not sufficient to assess the threat that wind turbines may pose to populations . . . but some of the same tree roosting and aerial feeding species that have been killed by wind turbines in other European countries also occur in the UK.

Other wildlife impacts

Birds and bats are specifically harmed by wind turbines because they are rapidly moving structures. Most other wildlife impacts are more general in cause and similar to those found when any major construction project damages natural and semi-natural habitats. Thus we find the great crested newt, badgers, polecats, red squirrels and many others listed in objections, whether to wind farms, factories or housing estates. In all these cases the final decision has to be a matter of cost/benefit but from all that has gone before, my own opinion is manifestly that no wind farm can be justified against the backdrop of environmental damage.

Because wind farms so often target upland plateaux they very often threaten peat-land habitats. Peat is the accumulated residue of many thousands of years of plant growth in conditions where water-logging prevents oxidation by limiting gaseous diffusion, and also very often because the acid soil inhibits bacterial breakdown of dead plants. Such peat areas are becoming rarer as a result of agricultural drainage, liming and fertilisation and as they are lost they take with them a living assemblage of specialist plants and animals, not to mention a remarkable stratified and preserved record of both archaeology and palaeo-biology. Much of what we know of Quaternary habitats and ecosystems has been pieced together from sub-fossil pollen and macro-fossil evidence from peat bogs.

Wind farm construction could not be better designed to damage the peat-lands of our country. Excavation for access roads interferes with and creates new routes for drainage and the import of huge amounts of crushed rock greatly modifies soil and drainage water chemistry, promoting both drying and bacterial oxidation of peat. At the time of construction there is also an almost uncontrollable increase of water-erosion and wind-erosion of peat, some of which has been dramatically displayed in Braes of Doune and Cefn Croes website photo collections. The most extreme damage to peat areas by wind turbine construction has literally resulted in landslides of the organic blanket, for example at Derrybrien in the Republic of Ireland.[10]

Many deep peat habitats represent a gigantic reservoir of stored carbon which has been fixed by thousands of years of photosynthesis and which is unable to return to the atmosphere because of wetness and acidity. We have already seen in Chapter 5 that the energy- and CO_2-payback time of wind farms may be massively extended if drainage and other construction damage allows this sequestered carbon to oxidize.

References and notes

1.   Appeal Decision, The Planning Inspectorate (27 December, 2007) Farmland adjacent to Skitfield Road, Guestwick, Norwich.
2.   IPCC 2007 Fourth Assessment Report. *Summary for Policy Makers.*

3.   http://www.esru.strath.ac.uk/EandE/Web_sites/03-04/wind/content/ukwindspeedmap.html

4.   McNeish, Cameron (April 2006) *Sunday Herald*.

5.   Appeal Decision (2008) against the decision of West Berkshire Council. Land at Baydon Meadow, Lambourn, Berkshire.

6.   *Natuur.Oriolus* 69 (3). (2003).

7.   Smallwood, K.S. and Thelander, C.G. (2004), Developing methods to reduce bird mortality in the Altamont Pass Wind Resource Area, Public Interest Energy Research Program Contract No. 500-01-019, *Final Report to the California Energy Commission*.

8.   Horn, Arnett & Kunz (2008) *Journal of Wildlife Management* 72(1):123–132.

9.   *New Scientist* (17:00 25 August, 2008) Wind turbines make bat lungs explode. [Erin Baerwald and her colleagues collected 188 dead bats from wind farms across southern Alberta. Ninety per cent of the bats had signs of internal haemorrhaging, but only half showed any signs of direct contact with the windmill blades. Only 8% had signs of external injuries but no internal injuries.

10. Radio Telefis Eireann RTE News (3 July, 2008).
     http://www.rte.ie/news/2008/0703/derrybrien.html
     [The European Court of Justice has ruled against Ireland in a case involving a wind farm project in Co Galway where a landslide killed 50,000 fish in 2003. The court said that a proper environmental impact assessment should have been carried out before the project proceeded.] And see for further details *The politics of peat* (2006). Scottish Wind Assessment Project.

7 Noise, shadows and flicker

> The sound of a wind turbine generating electricity is likely to be about the same level as noise from a flowing stream about 50-100 metres away or the noise of leaves rustling in a gentle breeze. (BWEA website)

> E.ON has today announced that it no longer intends to continue to develop an eight turbine wind farm near Ferndale because of concerns that the project's original design could potentially pose a noise nuisance to nearby homes. (Press release, 2 July, 2008)

Not all wind farms cause a problem of noise. Many earlier ones were remote from homes and their sound irritated only a few walkers and other users of the countryside, though even then there were complaints that quite distant machines made sufficient noise to disrupt sleep and cause annoyance during daytime. The situation is changing, however. As the developers have grabbed (or been denied) the remote lands of Britain, so their flailing blades perforce creep closer to habitations. The E.ON development, Ty'n Tyle wind farm, cited in the chapter header, is about a kilometre from each of the South Wales' valley communities of Ferndale and Ystrad. Many current developments will be at this sort of distance from homes, but denial is endemic: Gordon James, director of Friends of the Earth Cymru, dismissively responded to E.ON's release, "Noise isn't a problem . . . Modern wind turbines are very quiet."

Sound attenuates with distance from source by an approximate inverse square law so, if distance is halved, perceived noise increases by about four times. The remarkable push for renewable energy which has been imposed by the regional planning advice notes will allow many more turbines to be built close to habitation and there will thus be a growing impact of noise on human health, happiness and prosperity. This will all be done under the umbrella guidelines of the cryptically named ETSU-R-97[1] which was prepared by The Working Group on Noise from Wind Turbines comprising developers, noise consultants, environmental health officers and others set up by the DTI (now DBERR).

There are two potential sources of noise: that from turbine blades passing through the air at the speed of a light aircraft, and from the gearbox and generator in the nacelle. According to the industry, blade design can reduce the first problem of aerodynamic sound, whilst gear design, sound insulation and isolation suppresses mechanical noise. This is to an extent a clever exercise in concealment.

It is true that engineering can suppress mechanical noise but an aerofoil blade, the size of a Jumbo's wing, travelling at 150 mph and harvesting 0.6 MW of power or more, inevitably makes substantial sound! The air passing through the rotor is swept into turbulent wake-vortices, the source of much of the sound, and within a few feet encounters the obstruction of the tower. As a blade passes a tower every one to two seconds this imposes a pulsating quality to the aerodynamic sound which many people find deeply disturbing. Other periodic sounds arise as the blades sweep down into the region of wind shear so that the lowest blade position experiences not only different wind speed but also varying turbulence. It is a deliberate untruth that "Noise isn't a problem" and as we shall see ETSU-R-97 is not a fit instrument to assess it.

In the case of wind farm clusters of turbines there are further possibilities of interaction of sound periodicity. As the rotors of different machines come into and go out of phase, they can create periodic "beat" sounds (aerodynamic or amplitude modulation) allowing the rhythmic "whoomph, whoomph" at one to two second intervals to rise and fall in loudness, an effect which so disturbs some people. This sound is of low but audible frequency – comparable to the base – "woofer" speaker output of a sound system.

In addition to normally audible sound, any machinery will generate a degree of low frequency sound (effectively mechanical vibration) which ranges from just audible "sub-woofer" frequencies (below 200 Hz) down to wavelengths which cannot be heard but are often sensed as bodily discomfort (below 20 Hz) and are often referred to as infrasound which is particularly difficult to measure instrumentally. The industry and several independent reports claim that it is not a problem but this is controversial.

The measurement of noise

Noise is measured in decibels (dB). The decibel is a measure of the sound pressure level, i.e., the magnitude of the pressure variations in the air, expressed as a ratio to a reference pressure. The scale is logarithmic so an increase of 3 dB is a doubling of sound pressure. Measurements of environmental noise are usually made in dB(A) which includes a correction for the frequencies (different pitches), best-heard by the human ear. Unfortunately the A-weighting tends to devalue the low frequency end of the spectrum and has been criticised where low frequencies are important – repetitive base notes in music and of course the pervasive aerodynamic "whoomph" of wind turbines. The C- weighting curve is more satisfactory as it is less selective against low frequency but ETSU-R-97 mandates dB(A) as do many other sound measuring conventions.

The noise a wind turbine creates can be expressed in terms of its sound power level at source. This is a measure of the noise emitted by the machine and is also expressed in dB(A). BWEA claims that a single wind turbine usually emits between 90 and 100 dB(A) and creates a sound pressure level of 50-60 dB(A) at a distance of 40 metres from the turbine[2] and that:

> Ten such wind turbines, all at a distance of 500 metres
> would create a noise level of 35-45 dB(A) under the same

conditions. With the wind blowing in the opposite direction the noise level would be about 10 dB lower.

To put this in perspective some comparable noise sound pressure levels in dB(A) are:

Rural background:	20-40
Bedroom at night:	25
Quiet home interior:	35-40
Wind farm at 500 m:	35-45
Car at 40mph at 100 m:	55
Vestas V80 2 MW wind turbine close-up (wind 10 m/s):	98-99
Jet aircraft take-off at 100 m:	125

Use of the dB scale tends to confuse the lay person and this has been deliberately exploited in many of the wind industry's planning applications. In recent years several of these have been ruled inadequate. It is useful to know that in the open air, a change of 3 dB is barely discernable but a 5 dB change will cause most people to comment and a 10 dB increase, perceived as an approximate doubling of noise, will result in complaints from most people. The use of the dB(A) frequency scale, biased for human hearing, also implies that perception of sounds as unpleasant, neutral or pleasing, simply relates to loudness. This is not so, and one has to ask how a single noise-level reading relates to the range of subjective experiences described below which include periodic sounds, their variation in pitch (frequency) and vibrations close to the lowest audible frequency.

It has been noted that music and noise from discos and the like have a totally different sound character to either steady or sporadic sounds and an A-weighted level has been found to be "inappropriate to assessing the intrusion inside a dwelling from low frequency thumping bass" (noted in an acoustician's response to a proposed wind power station at Bald Hills, Victoria, Australia).

Throughout the UK wind farm noise is assessed in planning applications using the prescribed methodology of ETSU-R-97, which, supposedly, can be used to define the noise from wind turbines and thus protect wind farm neighbours.

The first stage is to measure prevailing background noise levels during day and night time periods at a sample of representative properties – those where noise is expected to be a problem.

The second stage is to use those measurements to generate maximum permissible day-and night-time noise levels which are set at a prescribed margin above background level – normally 5 dB(A) (or, in low noise environments, at recommended fixed levels). The margin is prescribed in ETSU-R-97 and the required levels that emerge from this stage of the process are entirely dependent upon the results of the background noise measurements.

The third stage is to predict the likely noise emissions from the turbines at each of the representative properties – using manufacturers' output specifications against local anemometric data, topography etc. This is supposed to provide assurance that the turbines will be capable of operating within the pre-established noise limits. They are thus produced solely for comparison with the background noise measurements. The comparison does help ensure that there will be adequate separation distances from places of habitation.

If the work is not conducted critically, problems arise. These include, not only the appropriateness of selected "representative" locations but also replicability. Measurements taken by the same person, using the same protocol, but on different dates, would very likely vary from each other. This is not a precise science.

The ease with which poor sound measurement can result in an injustice is illustrated by the Judicial Review of an Inquiry's findings concerning the Den Brook Valley Wind Farm in Devonshire. Renewable Energy Systems' (RES) appeal against refusal of permission for the wind farm was conceded on noise grounds alone but a Judicial Review in 2008 led the Secretary of State to quash the unlawful planning permission on another ground, namely that the planning inspector, as part of the overall planning balance must consider the likely electricity contribution of the particular site. The case set a precedent that wind farm neighbours have the right to raw environmental data and it is now beyond doubt that RES' noise assessment contained errors http://www.denbrookvalley.co.uk/

The appropriateness of ETSU-R-97 may be further judged from the comments by acoustic consultant Bowdler[3]:

> The conclusions of ETSU-R-97 are so badly argued as to be laughable in parts (the daytime standard is based on the principle that it does not matter if people cannot get to sleep on their patio so long as they can get to sleep in their bedrooms). It is the only standard where the permissible night time level is higher than the permissible day time level . . .

Bowdler further comments on Paragraph 1 of the Executive Summary of ETSU-R-97 that it clearly says:

> This document describes a framework for the measurement of wind farm noise and gives indicative noise levels thought to offer a reasonable degree of protection to wind farm neighbours, without placing unreasonable restrictions on wind farm development or adding unduly to the costs and administrative burdens on wind farm developers or local authorities.

Government is effectively saying "the debate is over" – an undemocratic and anti-science stance we have grown used to in other quarters of the climate change discussion. But the debate on noise does continue in technical publication, for example in van den Berg's recent investigation of Dutch wind farm of variable speed turbines (10 to 22 rpm). Complaints about noise, especially at night, extended to 1.9 km whereas the developer had claimed there would be no problem over 0.5 km.[4] Van den Berg showed that the night time wind speed at hub height is up to 2.6 times higher than expected from the conventional extrapolation from wind speed measured at 10 m height. The higher wind speed causes faster rotation and up to 15 dB higher sound levels, relative to the same 10 m reference wind speed in daytime. His paper also concluded that day or night, the background noise did not effectively mask the thumping sound of the blades passing the tower and interestingly observes that the thumping is not perceptible close to the turbines – only at a distance.

That discussion still continues is illustrated by a very recent publication from the independent consultants who sat on the 2006-7 DTI and BERR Noise Working Group.[5] Their paper attempts to arrive at a procedure for coping with the 10 m wind speed problem and site-specific wind shear (as described by van den Berg). In concurrence with van den Berg, this paper also concluded that the mismatch between 10 m and hub height wind measurements can cause significant errors in noise calculation. The Noise Working Group also revisited the matter of infra-sound and repeated the views which have come from others, that infrasound from wind turbines (less than 20 Hz) is not sufficiently energetic to be sensed by the human body. This is discussed further below.

Possibly the most publicised case of a wind turbine noise problem in Britain is that of the Davies family of Spalding in Lincolnshire.[6] When the construction of Deeping St Nicholas wind farm was proposed, just 930 m from their farmhouse, Julian and Jane Davis initially had no objection. However, after the eight 2.0 MW turbines became operational in summer 2007 the Davis's discovered that pervasive noise was intolerable.

> By May 2007 we were forced to abandon our home as a place in which to sleep and live.

The problem has been recognised as rendering the house valueless:

> I am not able to place a current market value on the property as I do not believe any prospective purchaser would want to inhabit the property, or, indeed in the current climate, whether any mortgage lender would be prepared to lend . . . (Munton & Russel, Estate Agents Spalding, April 2008)

The noise also triggered a Council Tax reduction by the Lincolnshire Valuation Tribunal which reduced the Grays Farm and adjacent Farmhouse from Band B to Band A with effect from June 2006 on the grounds of "Noise pollution externally and internal low frequency noise pollution from new wind farm 930m." Parliament has now been told that "proximity of a electricity generating wind turbine" can be the reason for a discretionary discount on Council Tax (*Hansard*, 13 May, 2008: Column 1442W ff). So much for "Noise isn't a problem . . ." – and when did silent "elegant and beautiful structures" last qualify property for a rates reduction?

I have spent some time on the Davis' case but there are many more examples. A victim of a wind farm in New Zealand wrote ". . . worst of all is the beat. An insidious, low-frequency vibration that's more a sensation than a noise. It defeats double-glazing and ear plugs, coming up through the ground, or through the floors of houses, and manifesting itself as a ripple up the spine, a thump on the chest or a throbbing in the ears. Those who feel it say it's particularly bad at night. It wakes them up or stops them getting to sleep." (Hawkes Bay Today [NZ], 18 February, 2006).

Many of these responses appear to be triggered by what has come to be known as aerodynamic modulation (AM) and the Davis's believe their experience at Deeping St Nicholas has that cause:

> We now know that we suffer from aerodynamic or amplitude modulation created by the noise from the wind turbine array. [which] is not fully understood by scientists. This means that no developer can categorically state that there will not be a noise problem.[6]

The Hayes-McKenzie report of 2006, commissioned by the DTI to investigate low frequency effects, noted that the main cause of complaints was not low frequency sound but Aerodynamic Modulation.[7] This can loosely be defined as audible modulation of aerodynamic noise, i.e. aerodynamic noise which displays a greater degree of fluctuation than usual and occasionally occurring in ways not anticipated by ETSU-R-97. The causes are not well understood but include the interaction of sound from more than one turbine and consequent reinforcement of sound pulses from the passing frequency of blades with both the tower and the wind shear zone lower in the swept circle of the rotor.

The Hayes-McKenzie report also stated that concerns about this phenomenon have been expressed in relation to only five out of 126 wind farms in the UK. Despite this, the DTI commissioned a further study of AM from the University of Salford which reported in 2007 that the incidence was low but even so, concluded:

> On the other hand, since AM cannot be fully predicted at present, and its causes are not understood we consider that it might be prudent to carry out further research to improve understanding in this area.[8]

The official response to this advice whilst the Davis's languished in rented accommodation was:

> Government does not consider there to be a compelling case for further work into AM and will not carry out any further research at this time.

A recent report from the Noise Association[9] (NA) certainly recognises a generalised noise problem for some people, living less than 1 to 1.5 miles from a turbine, and that not all individuals are equally affected.

For people who cannot shut out the noise, the problem can be exacerbated by the rotating blades and the dancing shadows of turbines so that noise from turbines can be much more intrusive that other noises of a similar decibel level.

The report also notes that, for those who are sensitive, the impact of turbines can be overwhelming and a particular problem in quiet rural areas. Low-frequencies may form an audible but not major part of turbine noise and can create additional problems for some but the infrasound content of wind turbine noise is too low to affect most people. However, low frequency may be underestimated because of the persistent use of "A" weighting in measuring the noise, rather than taking "C" weighted measurements. Some medical reports include persistent complaints from people saying they not only hear the noise from wind turbines, but can "feel" disturbance in their bodies, leading to symptoms similar to those associated with vibro-acoustic disease (VAD). This latter observation is in slight conflict with the NA's previous suggestion that infrasound content is too low to have clinical effect and it is worth looking further at the industry's and Government's current stance on low frequency noise.

Sounds below the frequency range for human hearing have been the subject of ongoing controversy in the context of wind power. The BWEA has consequently felt need to provide a web-page on the subject http://www.bwea.com/ref/lowfrequencynoise.html which reports:

Dr Geoff Leventhall, Consultant in Noise Vibration and Acoustics and author of the Defra Report on Low Frequency Noise and its Effects, says: 'I can state quite categorically that there is no significant infrasound from current designs of wind turbines.'

However, a report from Keele University on infrasound[10] says:

> We have clearly shown that both fixed speed and variable
> speed turbines generate low frequency vibrations which are
> multiples of blade passing frequencies and can be detected
> by seismometers buried in the ground

Detection was possible at distances up to many kilometres and in the presence of background seismic noise. In the absence of peer-reviewed medical evidence concerning low frequency sound from wind turbines, these two statements make uncomfortable bedfellows and so, as with many other aspects of this industry, we have a "Catch 22" in which proof of a problem can only come when it is too late. However it is significant that the few medical workers looking at low-frequency noise from wind turbines on three continents are in agreement to the extent of christening the health consequence "Wind Turbine Syndrome"[11] and now in a forthcoming book of eponymous title. The syndrome includes sleep disturbance, headache, dizziness, nausea, rapid heart rate, panic attacks and significantly, if the families Pierpont studied moved away from the turbines (sometimes abandoning their homes), the symptoms, significantly, went away.

The BWEA followed-up the publication of the Keele University report with a rebuttal of any suggestion that infrasound was a health issue. In this rebuttal two of the original authors, Styles and Toon, wrote:

> To put the level of vibration into context, they are ground
> vibrations with amplitudes of about one millionth of a
> millimetre. There is no possibility of humans sensing the
> vibration and absolutely no risk to human health.

However, a more recent development has been the publication in 2008 of a study which has shown for the first time that the human vestibular system is also extremely sensitive to low-frequency and infrasound vibrations by making use of a new technique for measuring vestibular activation.[12]

Perturbation of the vestibular apparatus is a core response underlying Pierpont's Wind Turbine Syndrome. This demonstration of extreme sensitivity to low frequency vibration suggests that Styles and Toon's dismissive "no possibility of humans sensing the vibration" may not be correct and that government's refusal to commission further work is, at the least, premature. Coupled with recent findings by Alves-Pereira & Branco that "In-Home Wind Turbine Noise Is Conducive to Vibroacoustic Disease"[13] this appears to support the former Dean of Medicine at the University of Western Ontario who is calling for health studies into the wind turbine farms being built in the State and suggests that if there is enough evidence, a formal epidemiological study should be made.[14] Alves-Pereira & Branco's conclusion was that infrasound and low frequency noise generated by WT blades can lead to severe health problems, specifically, VAD, and efficient zoning for WT must be scientifically determined, and quickly adopted, in order that Public Health may be properly protected.

Perception

In no part of the confrontation between the wind power industry and people have there been more attempts at misrepresentation than in relation to noise and visual intrusion. The following quotations from Pedersen & Waye's (2005) paper to the 1st International Meeting on Wind Turbine Noise sums up the subjective feelings of countless people, that exposure to wind turbine noise, shadows and the rotating movement of the rotor blades, were an intrusion into the "private domain".

The wind turbine noise was by some of the informants perceived as intruding into private domain, physically into

> the garden and the home, but also as intruder into themselves.

> The experience of lacking control, being subjected to injustice, lacking influence, and/or not being believed.

> The noise . . . was to those who could not mentally shut it out, an obstacle to pleasant experiences decreasing the joy of daily life at home . . . creating a feeling of violation that was expressed as anger, uneasiness, and tiredness.

That such feelings are not amenable to interpretation by noise metering is the crux of the problem. A dripping tap making a sound near the lower threshold of hearing can be more infuriating than the continuous hum of traffic on a nearby road.

> As the science of acoustics has developed, sociological surveys have become an important aspect in developing noise criteria. These surveys, combined with accurate measurements of the noise, enable a reliable assessment of the percentage of people likely to be annoyed to be developed.[15]

The setting of levels in ETSU-R-97 in no way made this sort of approach. It does appear to be true that a significant proportion of people are much more seriously affected by noise than others. In our twenty-first century society a similar proportion of people also suffer from a range of disabilities which reduce the quality of their lives and Government has been wise in making it a legal requirement that such unfortunates should not be prevented from leading a normal life. However, the same government has engendered a subsidy system without which wind turbines could not be built. The consequence is that a sensitive minority may be tormented by the legal, but in my view quite unreasonable, activity of wind power developers.

Unfortunately, despite 20 years of complaint about noise, most of the evidence is still dismissed by government as apocryphal and it will remain true that there is little clinical evidence until proper independent research is financed. The repeated reference to compliance with ETSU-R-97 which appears in countless government statements and planning documents is little more than an escape clause. The noise problem of wind turbines, both modulation effects and low frequency sound, is not addressed by the provisions of ETSU-R-97 and the document seems not to be a fit instrument for purpose.

I close this account of wind farm noise with sympathy for the thousands of people, worldwide, who could write, as has the Marton, Askam & Ireleth Windfarm Action Group (MAIWAG):

> The windfarm is noisy, it is a visual blight, it does create shadow flicker, it has resulted in very little benefit to the local economy, it has not resulted in an increase in tourism and negotiating with PowerGen Renewables and Wind Prospect to try to resolve the problems has been a most unpleasant experience for all those involved. Simply put, we want our quality of life back.
>
> (http://www.windfarm.fsnet.co.uk/index.htm)

Shadow flicker, reflection and silhouetting

Shadow flicker occurs when the sun passes behind the hub of a wind turbine and shadows of the rotating blades pass repeatedly over neighbouring properties. The seasonal timing and duration of flicker can be calculated from the geometry of the turbine, its orientation relative to nearby houses and the latitude of the site. Quite detailed information and a calculator are given on the Danish Wind Industry Association (DWIA) website.[16] Wind power developers claim to use commercially available software to minimise the risk of shadow flicker affecting homes. According to the DBERR website, flicker "has only been recorded occasionally at one site in the UK. The effect must depend to some extent on regulation of "set-back" – the permitted distance between turbines and homes which is a matter for the local planning authority in the UK.

Investigations of light flicker and photosensitive epilepsy suggest that there is a relatively low risk, as the flicker rate from a typical three-blade turbine is below three per second, i.e., sixty revolutions per minute, but the public should be protected from viewing interacting blades where the shadows cast by one turbine on another cause a cumulative flicker rate exceeding three per second and also to reduce this risk, turbine blades should not be reflective. Flicker rate is not affected by distance so any risk does not decrease significantly until it exceeds about 100 times the hub height – about 10 km for a big turbine.[17]

DBERR's comment on flicker is more cavalier:

> At a distance of 10 rotor diameters (equivalent to 400 to 800 metres) a person should not perceive a wind turbine to be chopping through sunlight.[18]

These findings are however supported by Epilepsy Action which reports that it has never received a call from anyone who believes they have had a seizure as a result of a wind turbine.

When turbines are geographically placed so they are visible from homes or valuable view-points, with either the early morning or the low evening sun behind them, they may become very much more prominent by silhouetting, and in these circumstances attempts to reduce their landscape impact such as DWIA's recommendation of grey painting are valueless. It is also in these circumstances that wind turbines draw the eye and become an irritation in the landscape. The Inspector at a Guestwick (Norfolk) planning Inquiry acknowledged this:

> I consider that the dominance of the turbine towers and the visual prominence of the blades, particularly when in

motion, would have a much more serious adverse effect than the appellants' witness claimed.

A much earlier planning inquiry into a proposed wind farm at Jordanston, Pembrokeshire (2000) included this:

> The movement of WTGs [wind turbine generators]... has a discordant effect on the eye. The rotation of the blades of WTGs in a cluster, while in the same direction, is not synchronised and gives a constant restless quality to the overall experience of a landscape. Especially when several overlapping WTGs are in view at one time.

Reflective flashing or enhanced visibility occurs when the sun is behind or slightly to the side of the observer and again accentuates the irritation caused by the moving blades.

To suggest, as does DWIA, that wind turbines are "natural elements in the landscape" or as journalist Polly Toynbee once wrote, "the gentle turning of these silent white wings delights more people than it offends" is beyond belief for any lover of the countryside who has the slightest inkling that wind turbines do virtually nothing for the supposed objective of stabilising or reducing atmospheric CO_2. They are money factories which industrialise the landscape for no other significant purpose.

References and Notes.

1. ETSU-R-97 (Assessment and Rating of Noise from Wind Farms) (1997). Prepared for Government by The Working Group on Noise from Wind Turbines. Department of Trade and Industry's Energy Technology Support Unit (ETSU).
2. BWEA website http://www.bwea.com/ref/noise.html
3. (a) Bowdler, R. (2005) ETSU-R-97 *Why it is Wrong* (Whinash Inquiry).
   (b) Bowdler, R. (2007) *Moorsyde Wind Farm Comments on the Noise Section of the Environmental Statement and other Documents*.

4. Van den Berg, G. P. (2004) Effects of the wind profile at night on wind turbine sound. *Journal of Sound and Vibration*, 277, 955–970

5. Bowdler, R, Bullmore A et al (2009) Prediction and assessment of wind turbine noise. *Acoustics Bulletin*, March-April.

6. Davis, J & J (2008) evidence to the House of Lords House of Lords Select Committee on Economic Affairs 4th Report of Session 2007–08 *The Economics of Renewable Energy Volume II: Evidence*.

7. Hayes McKenzie (2006) The Measurement of Low Frequency Noise at Three UK Wind Farms.
    http://www.berr.gov.uk/whatwedo/energy/sources/renewables/explained/wind/onshore-offshore/page31267.html

8. University of Salford (2007) *Research into Aerodynamic Modulation of Wind Turbine Noise*.

9. Noise Association (2006). *Location, location, location*.

10. Styles, Simpson, et al (2005) *Microseismic and Infrasound Monitoring of Low Frequency Noise and Vibration from Windfarms*. Keele University.

11. Pierpont, N. (2006). Wind Turbine Syndrome. And a forthcoming book of the same name http://www.windturbinesyndrome.com/?page_id=932

12. Todd, Rosengren & Colebatch (2008) Tuning and sensitivity of the human vestibular system to low-frequency vibration. *Neuroscience Letters* 444 36–41.

13. Mariana Alves-Pereira & Nuno A. A. Castelo Branco (2007) In-Home Wind Turbine Noise Is Conducive to Vibroacoustic Disease. *Second International Meeting on Wind Turbine Noise*. Lyon, France.

14. *The London Free Press* (1 February, 2009) Doctor calls for health studies on windmill farms.
    http://lfpress.ca/newsstand/News/2009/02/01/8228966.html

15. Evidence from Graeme E Harding & Associates, retained by the Tarwin Valley Coastal Guardians to advise on proposed wind power station at Bald Hills.

16. Danish Wind Industry Association (DWIA) Guided Tour.
    http://www.windpower.org/composite-85.htm

17. Harding et al (2008) Wind turbines, flicker, and photosensitive epilepsy: Characterizing the flashing that may precipitate seizures and optimizing guidelines to prevent them.
    http://www3.interscience.wiley.com/journal/120084200/abstract?CRETRY=1&SRETRY=0

18. DBERR Flicker.
    http://www.berr.gov.uk/energy/sources/renewables/planning/onshore-wind/shadow-flicker/page18736.html

8 Danger and nuisance

"Anger is only one letter short of danger." (Anon)

Wind power is one of the few industrial processes in which the public can approach very closely and even touch operating plant. It is indeed sold on the basis that the land below can still be used, especially for farming. Many of the upland and coastal areas which have been targeted by the developers are criss-crossed by public rights of way and some have also been opened to access by recent "right to roam" legislation.

The rotor of a big turbine weighs in excess of 30 tonnes. These are the largest rotating structures ever built and almost none of the bigger machines (2 MW and over) have operated yet for even a third of their life-expectation, thus as the turbines age, fatigue failure is an unknown quantity though blade-loss or -breakage are already the commonest mechanical problems. Such accidents are documented in detail by the Caithness Windfarm Information Forum[1] (CWIF) which also shows that the numbers of accidents are increasing as wind installed capacity grows.

A single turbine blade can be 10 tonnes in weight and as it is aerodynamically shaped, blades or broken bits can fly in the wind and a whole blade would be akin to a fighter aircraft crashing. The blades of the huge Enercon E112 turbine, the shape of things to come, weigh 20 tonnes each! In future, because government is promoting the concept of "brownfield" wind farms occupying urban and industrial sites, wind turbines will move ever closer to habitations, workplaces and recreational areas. Pieces of blade have been recorded travelling over 400m, and usually from much smaller turbines than those proposed for use today.[1] This is why CWIF believes that there should be a minimum distance of at least 2 km between turbines and occupied housing, to address public safety and also issues of noise and shadow flicker.

The second most frequent accident is fire, usually fed by hundreds of litres of lubricating oil from the transmission train oil-baths. Because of the height, fire fighting equipment cannot reach to the top of the tower so the fire brigade can do little but wait for fire to burn out.

The possible consequence of fire has recently been highlighted by an accident to a 0.66 MW turbine at the Nissan motor works in Sunderland (UK). All three 75 foot blades burned through and dropped onto the factory site. There are serious implications for siting of turbines in fire-prone forestry or amongst refinery buildings (*Sunderland Today*, 24 December, 2005). Fire is generally caused by faults in the transmission train or wind-shaft braking system and the Sunderland accident was attributed to a loose bolt and frictional heating).

In windy conditions burning debris may be scattered over a wide area, with obvious consequences, especially as many wind farms are in areas of naturally fire prone vegetation such as moorland, scrub or forest land. A typical example was reported in *Adelaide Now*, 3 February, 2009, when a large wind turbine caught fire near Port Lincoln and falling fragments started spotfires on the ground.

The possibilities of failure are well recognised by insurance companies and an inspection clause has been included in contracts since 2002. Rotor blades and their internal lightning protection must be inspected once a year and after 40,000 operating hours (or five years), must be reconditioned. The gears, generator and main bearings must also be replaced after 40,000 operating hours, regardless of their condition, and the stator and rotor windings of the generator and the gear wheels must be examined. It is quite clear that these requirements are a significant additional cost factor.[2]

In common with aircraft wings, wind turbine blades are prone to icing in freezing conditions. This causes production losses from wind turbines and heavy icing can close-down turbines as automatic controls sense growing imbalance of the rotor. Several weeks' lost production in a single icing incident have been reported in Southern Germany and ice thrown off the blades may also pose a safety risk even in areas where icing is infrequent, specifically when the turbines are situated close to a public road, or by skiing resorts, for example.

Ice shedding from the tower or the nacelle can also pose a similar though more limited risk especially for the service personnel and the public. There are also cases when icing of the yaw gear has resulted in the damage of the yawing motor.[3]

In the UK icing is a winter hazard in upland areas and occurs less frequently in the lowlands, but in the "unexpectedly" cold winter of 2008-9 people and parked cars in King's Dyke, Whittlesey (Cambridgeshire), were showered with huge lumps of ice, some two feet long, from a 260ft high turbine on an industrial estate close to homes and customer parking areas.[4] A piece of ice no more than the size of a butter pack falling from 200 feet would be a lethal missile. The failure was blamed on a faulty sensor, intended to halt the rotor when temperatures fall.

Much publicity has been given by the wind power industry to the continued use for recreation and agriculture which wind power makes possible. Indeed BWEA's state of the industry report *Wind Energy in the UK* (2008) features a whole-page photograph of young people mountain-biking through a wind farm. Uncomfortably for these cosy recreational predictions, many site operators have recently erected warning signs. At Crystal Rig for example:

> BE AWARE OF THE FOLLOWING HAZARDS. HIGH VOLTAGE ELECTRICITY (33 KV) DANGER OF DEATH. SNOW AND ICE FALLING FROM THE BLADES AND TOWERS . . .

And Cambrian Wind Energy's Cefn Croes wind farm:

DO NOT APPROACH TURBINES IN ADVERSE WEATHER
CONDITIONS, PARTICULARLY LIGHTNING STORMS OR IN COLD
CONDITIONS WHEN ICE COULD FORM.

At Mynydd Clogau wind farm near Newtown in Powys a "Right
to Roam" sign is overprinted with a cancellation symbol – and so
it goes on. If you still wish to visit these despoiled uplands you will
be warned off.

The opposition group SHWAG (Seamer & Hilton Windfarm
Action Group) has compiled a useful synopsis of wind power
hazards in the UK and concluded not surprisingly, that no one is
looking after public safety. Neither the Developers, the Local
Planning Authorities, the Highways Agency, the Local Highways
Authority, the National Grid nor the Health and Safety Executive
assess the risks to the public during the progressing of a planning
application.[5]

Aircraft safety and lighting

In 2006 I wrote that warning lights are required on onshore
structures "exceeding 150 m in height"[6] but there were no turbines
of that size in the UK at the time. Also, offshore wind turbines, out
to the seaward limits of the territorial water and which are 60 m or
more above the level of the sea at the highest tide, require at least
one medium intensity steady red light as close as possible to the
top of the fixed structure. Arrays of turbines require only peripheral
machines to be lit.[7]

However matters have now changed onshore, and the height
limit has effectively been abandoned so that any turbine could be
required to have a light on the top of its nacelle:

> [The] Ministry of Defence (MoD) have reviewed their
> aviation lighting requirements for wind turbines. In the
> interest of Air Safety we now request that the turbines are
> lit with 25 candela omni-directional red lighting at the
> highest practical point . . . The MOD will continue to

assess the need for aviation lighting on a case by case basis . . . We are also in the process of trialling 18 candela Infra Red lighting which is invisible to the naked eye . . . it is not always necessary for each turbine to be lit but attaching lights to those turbines defining the corners of a wind farm may be sufficient. (Letter from MoD to the Planning Inspectorate dated 13 February 2009, concerning practices for maintaining safety of aircrew engaged in low flying.)

Television, telecommunications and radar

Television. Large buildings and other structures such as wind farms can disrupt terrestrial television reception. Any structure will produce two zones of potential disruption to reception. One zone is where the development creates a "shadow", so weakening the signal and the other where it gives a "reflection". This causes multipath effects, where there is corruption or distortion of the received signal by the secondary signal often causing ghosting – multiple images.

Uniquely with wind turbines, rotating blades may "chop" the signal causing variable "ghosting" or "jittering" on an analogue TV picture. Analogue reception is more likely to be affected than digital terrestrial reception, which is more robust, but picture degradation linked with the construction of masts, towers, wind-turbines, and buildings is unfortunately common and both analogue and digital terrestrial reception can be affected.[8] A poor analogue picture can often still be viewed but a digital signal is either very good or so bad that it suffers digital break up into pixels and is impossible to watch.

The effects of wind power on broadcast television are generally found where the wind farm is situated between the TV and the transmitter, with reception being affected up to a distance of about 5 km.[8] A useful rule of thumb is that if the proposed wind farm significantly modifies the sky-line seen from a home, then there is the possibility that it may cause television reception difficulties at that location.[8] Modern composite turbine blades have less reflective effect than older metal rotors but embedded lightning conductor strips may negate this advantage. Reception solutions may need a more directionally sensitive aerial or aiming it at a different transmitter, though this is not always possible in remote and hilly areas. More expensive remedies may need a re-broadcasting mast, satellite or cable supply to affected householders.

Because extensive deployment of wind farms is happening simultaneously with the switch to digital TV in the UK, it is too early to predict whether reception problems will continue, but needless to say, the developers claim digital will be the solution. For example Renewable Energy Systems (RES) said in environmental statement documents, recently submitted to Devonshire County Council:

> The advent of digital services is also expected to minimise
> such problems.

This also appears in advice to government from the Sustainable Development Commission (SDC):

> In the future, the switch from analogue to digital terrestrial
> television may mean that transmission networks become
> less vulnerable to interference from wind developments.[9]

Disturbingly the industry and its proponents also suggest solutions to TV interference problems which reduce freedom of choice of services. For example the SDC wrote of problems at Blaen Bowi in Carmarthenshire:

> In some cases, the installation of satellite TV at affected
> households is an alternative option.[9]

The predicted life of a wind farm is 20-25 years. Is the SDC suggesting that the developer might commit to a pay-service for this time? – assuming that the wind farm is not sold-on in the meantime as happens so often in this entrepreneurial market – and indeed has at Blaen Bowi.

Telecommunications. The main issue with wind turbines is the multi-path effect, where there is corruption or distortion of the received signal as discussed for TV. The main effect is on fixed radio links which carry trunk telephone services, mobile phone services, TV, government and defence communications etc . . . mostly at microwave frequencies and over large distances. The wind turbine clearance zones around point-to-point microwave links are however quite narrow and clearance zones can be calculated and provided.

The water and power industries use scanning telemetry systems to monitor and control substations, water and sewage works, pipelines and supply networks. These systems work in the UHF band and are more vulnerable to multi-path effects from reflecting objects such as wind turbines, thus needing larger clearance zones and posing a more serious problem which in some cases is not easily soluble.[9]

Military remote sensing may also be compromised by effects other than reflection of electromagnetic waves. The seismic monitoring of international compliance with the Comprehensive Test Ban Treaty may be jeopardised as wind turbines may generate low frequency and infrasound vibration which can prevent detection of the seismic signals from nuclear weapons tests (see Chapter 7).

Aviation and military radar

> Aviation and radar issues have long been a major source of complaint for the wind industry. This is because wind turbines can interfere with radar systems and be a collision risk for low-flying aircraft. These concerns have resulted in a significant number of planning objections, particularly from the Ministry of Defence.[9]

Developers are able to submit pre-planning enquiries to Defence Estates and out of the 4,000 pre-planning consultation requests received since 1996, around 2,000 have received "no objections" advice. In total nearly half of the wind farms proposed so far in Britain have been successfully opposed by the MoD because of their proximity to air-defence, according to David Wallace, vice-president, Royal Society (*Nature*, 428, 2004).

The main effect of wind turbines on air-traffic control radar is due to the rotation of the blades. The radar may "illuminate" one turbine on one sweep, then a different one on the next sweep, producing shifting radar returns sometimes referred to as "twinkling" on the radar screen. Usually this only occurs when the wind development is within a line of sight (LOS) of the radar. In June 2003 Defence Estates agency of the MoD wrote in a letter to Aberdeenshire Council:

> [The] decision was made to object to any wind energy development that was within line of sight and 74 km of an Air Defence Radar.

In 2005 three trial reports on effects on radar were issued by the Air Warfare Centre of the RAF[10] from which the following are extracts:

> 6 January, 05 It was confirmed that on the T101 radar, primary radar returns from aircraft having a low Radar Cross Section (Hawk T Mk 1a and Tucano T Mk 1) are lost when flying over wind turbines, regardless of the aircraft's height . . . the MoD has provisionally ceased automatic approval of wind turbine developments beyond 74 km but within Line of Sight from an AD radar.

> 10 May, 05 Throughout the Trial, clutter was displayed to the operator as a result of the motion of the wind turbines.

This displayed clutter was assessed as highly detrimental to
the safe provision of Air Traffic Services (ATS).

It is recommended that: a. Planning applications for wind
turbine farm developments be subject to scrutiny when in
LoS of an airfield primary radar, regardless of range but in
particular within 30nm of the radar head.

12 Aug 05 It is recommended that the MoD continues to
examine closely the potential impact of any application for
a wind turbine farm within radar LoS of an AD radar,
regardless of range.

The creation of total "holes" in radar cover (6 January) and the
cluttering of radar screens with a "highly detrimental" effect on
safety, both caused by wind farms, is a matter of some concern!

In 2008 DBERR published a commissioned report entitled
Resolution of Radar Operation Objections To Wind Farm Developments
which opens with the comment "The BWEA has estimated that in
excess of 2 Giga-Watts of renewable energy potential could be
released if solutions are found." General findings were that the
ADT [Advanced Digital Tracker system] has been shown to be
effective at removing unwanted wind farm returns from the
operators' screens and it has been shown to effectively track aircraft
over wind farm areas.

Without further comment I record two press comments:

11 August, 2008. The Ministry of Defence has finally
withdrawn its objections to two major wind farms following
the intervention of Gordon Brown. For years the MoD has
fought the creation of two large wind farms off the coast of
Northumberland and Norfolk because of fears of radar
interference. It emerged last year that nearly half of all
proposed wind farms were stuck in the planning process

because of objections from the MoD, which has many RAF bases on the east coast of Britain. This meant that the Government had no chance of achieving its target of producing 20% of the country's total energy from renewable resources by 2020.[11]

11 December, 2008. NATS [National Air Traffic Service] said that the local terrain and the construction of large wind turbines had the potential to cause false primary surveillance radar (PSR) plots to be generated on the company's radar at Lowther Hill. It said: "Whilst a limited number of these false plots may be acceptable, NATS has concerns about the proliferation and impact of a large number of wind farms. Should all the wind farms currently in the planning system be built, this would unacceptably limit our ability to provide a safe and efficient air traffic service."[12]

According to BWEA's 2008 document *Aviation Structure & Memorandum of Understanding*, during a speech in advance of the Bali summit the Prime Minister asked the Secretaries of State for Defence, Transport and Business to:

. . . step up their efforts in cooperation with industry and the regulators to identify and test technical solutions to the potential difficulties that wind farms pose to air traffic and defence radar.

As a layman it worries me that, with a bit of political leaning we have gone in a few short years from radar interference being a serious problem to potential solutions to this complex safety problem.

This discussion has largely concerned military operations, radar and air traffic control but the effect of wind turbines on air safety may also be considerable if wind turbines are proposed near civilian airports. Anyone faced with a planning application in such circumstances would be well-advised to read the comments made by the planning inspectorate in comparable cases. A recent example was Ecotricity's application for five 120 m turbines at Langdon, near Dover which has recently been rejected at an appeal[13] in which the Inspector devoted more than 5 pages of deliberation to the aviation impact.

Kent International Airport (KIA) is some 20 km north of the proposed wind farm and the small Inglenook Farm airfield would be only 2.2 km from the nearest turbine. A navigation beacon is also about 2.3 km from the turbines and as a result of flight paths relative to the turbines and KIA its position could not be worse.

The proximity of turbines to Inglenook Farm airfield is a possible source of turbulence and risk to aircraft. A Civil Aviation Authority (CAA) letter concerning the application said that the effects of wind turbulence on aircraft are not yet known but pointed out that disturbed air is likely to return to free flow within 20 rotor diameters, in the worst case (1.64km) compared with the actual 2.2 km separation. The Inspector's response was that safety concerns relating to turbulence remain unresolved and may not be satisfactorily overcome.

A further problem is the CAA advice against obstacles greater than 150 feet within 2,000m of the runway centre. In this case, the nearest turbine would be slightly closer than 2,000m, but the turbine blade tips would also be some 460 feet higher than the runway. The decision to reject the appeal was based on "policy, safety and environmental" issues – safety essentially concerning the aviation issues.

Interference with radar and remote sensing is not the only problem for military aircraft. Wind generators are now reaching 140m (500 feet) above ground level. This is not high compared to the normal flying height of most aircraft but for some it is. The military practise low flying for operational reasons (ground support and flying "under the radar"). Standard heights are 250 or 300 feet (Civil aircraft typically operate at 1,000 feet around aerodromes except for approach and departure). The report on aviation for the DTI, is a useful further source of information.[14]

References and notes

1.   Caithness Windfarm Information Forum (2008). http://www.caithnesswindfarms.co.uk/accidents.pdf

2.   *Windblatt* (2002): The ENERCON Magazine, Issue 06.

3.   http://virtual.vtt.fi/virtual/arcticwind/index.htm

4.   Peterborough UK *Evening Telegraph*. http://www.peterboroughtoday.co.uk/news/Wind-turbine39s-deadly-ice-shower.4750005.jp?CommentPage=3&CommentPageLength=10

5.   http://www.shwag.co.uk/

6.   Etherington, J. R. (2006) *The Case against Wind Farms*. Country Guardian web site.

7.   Directorate of Airspace Policy (2003) *The Lighting of Offshore Wind Turbines*.

8.   BBC & Ofcom (2006) *The Impact of Large Buildings and Structures (including Wind Farms) on Terrestrial Television Reception*.

9.   Sustainable Development Commission (SDC) (2005) *Windpower in the UK*.

10. RAF (2005) Air Warfare Centre Open Reports. The Effects of Wind Turbine Farms on ATC Radar.

11. *This is Money* (11 August, 2008).

12. *Evening News and Star* (West Cumbria) 11 December, 2008. Windfarms now a threat to air safety.

13. Appeal Decision, The Planning Inspectorate (2009) Land near Langdon. Dover. Ecotricity Group Ltd application for 5 wind turbines up to 120m high – unsuccessful appeal against Dover District Council.

14. Jago, P & Taylor N (2002) *Wind Turbines and Aviation Interests European Experience and Practice*. ETSU W/14/00624/REP DTI.

9 Property, tourism and employment

I do not believe any prospective purchaser would want to inhabit the property, or, indeed in the current climate, whether any mortgage lender would be prepared to lend . . ."
(Munton & Russel, Estate Agents, Spalding, 2008)

It is no more than a matter of common sense that wind power may seriously affect property price. Given two identical rural houses, one with wind turbines on its horizon, in which would you invest two or three hundred thousand pounds? There is but one answer unless "green" commitment has displaced all caution. The chapter header tells the real story of what happened to the home of the Davis family in Lincolnshire.[1] And yet our Government promotes the DBERR web page which identifies it as a myth that "Wind farms devastate house prices"[2]

Have you ever noticed that the BBC2 television programme *Escape to the Country* almost never shows the splendid homes which it features as being anywhere near a wind farm – even when they are? Indeed those words are rarely mentioned and yet traffic noise is often invoked – or even "remoteness" – as an objection to purchasing.

A study of members' opinions by the Royal Institution of Chartered Surveyors (RICS) in 2004 concluded that:

60% of the sample suggested that wind farms decrease the value of residential properties where the development is within view . . . [and that] Once a wind farm is completed, the negative impact on property values continues but becomes less severe after two years or so after completion.[3]

The DBERR Myths website[2] misrepresents these findings: "A study by the Royal Institution of Chartered Surveyors suggests that wind farms have no lasting impact on UK house prices" and DBERR continues "It shows that local house prices recover from any initial impact once a wind farm has been operating for two years."

Compare "prices recover from any initial impact" with the very different original versions "negative impact . . . continues". This seems to be dishonest selling!

DBERR Myths then compounds the offence by writing "People promoting fears of falling prices risk making them self-fulfilling."

I am sure that this was not the interpretation arrived at by the district judge who awarded substantial compensation to a family from Marton in Cumbria, because a vendor failed to disclose a wind farm proposal![4]

A valuer in mid-Wales has suggested a probable 25% reduction in house value caused by a proposed wind farm[5] while in Devonshire, two independent valuers predicted that a bungalow would lose £165,000, a third of its value.[6] In this case one agent confirmed that the plan is "not going to help many properties within a mile of it" and added: "People move to the area for its beauty".

The wind power industry vehemently denies such impacts but facts and common sense speak louder than their words. The appalling story of the Davis family's experience with the Deeping St Nicholas wind farm in Lincolnshire first became public in an article in *Farmers Weekly* in early 2007[7] and has subsequently been outlined in the family's evidence to the House of Lords.[8]

The deeply disturbing thing is that the wind power industry refutes this evidence by saying there is no "proof" of impact on house prices, but unfortunately this is a classic Catch-22 situation in which the proof is the damnation – it will be too late when we know. It is also disturbing that a subsequent survey was conducted by the RICS in conjunction with Oxford-Brookes University which has been used to claim that there was no relationship between proximity to wind turbines and property value.[9]

The RICS-OBU survey took in just two small wind farms in Cornwall, St Breocks and St Eval with turbines about 50 m in total height – a half to a third the size of current models. The authors' first conclusion was that:

> There was a decline of about 50% in the value of semi-detached and terraced properties within 1 mile of the wind farm compared with those over 1.5 miles away. [And] The effect seems much less marked – if at all – for detached houses.

However the authors explained away their own major finding by suggesting that houses close to the wind farm in St Eval were ex-Ministy of Defence, and less desirable, but they made no statistical attempt to separate these two factors. As a further failing of methodology, no record was made of turbines being within sight of the homes, neither was it considered important that the huge demand for property in this area might significantly level the value.

The authors closed this flawed report, slightly redeeming themselves by suggesting that:

> [This] is only one study, and as more wind farms are built, more property will become proximate. Therefore, a cautious approach should be adopted until a larger and more in-depth study can be undertaken.

Despite this the wind industry now cites the study as evidence that property price is not harmed, for example, from a Force 9 publicity handout:

> One of the most recent studies on the effect of wind farms on house prices was undertaken in 2007 by Oxford Brookes

University, on behalf of the Royal Institute of Chartered Surveyors... For this reason developers cannot guarantee that the value of your home will not change, but the evidence shows that it certainly is not the average response for house prices to fall with the installation of a nearby wind farm. In fact, some studies actually find evidence to the contrary.[10]

If this were not so important to the average home owner and mortgage holder, such misuse of a totally inadequate survey to claim that black is white would be laughable. The suggestion that a nearby wind farm increases a property price can only be treated with the same contempt one must have for the view that:

The gentle turning of these silent white wings delights more people than it offends (journalist Polly Toynbee)

Tourism and employment

Just as common sense predicts that wind power will influence property price, it is also apparent that it will deflect the rural tourist who comes for peace and quiet, to escape the constant movement and noise of the city and to recharge their mental batteries.

Whether we like it or not, tourism is the future for rural Britain, and as Foot & Mouth disease sadly revealed some years ago, it is a substantially larger earner than agriculture. The following figures were compiled for Wales several years ago, but proportions will remain the same and be similar for Scotland and England.

Tourism earns almost £2 to £3 billion a year for Wales. It contributes 7% to Welsh GDP and far outweighs agriculture, at less than 2%. Tourism is much more cost-effective in terms of jobs, than agriculture, which becomes less labour intensive each year. Farms, which employed a dozen men 50 years ago, are often run on a man and his wife these days.

The conventional electricity industry contributes less than 2% to Welsh GDP and if the 2010 renewable generation target of 10% is achieved, it would represent, at best, 0.2% of the country's GDP.

Thus we have a thriving and rapidly growing tourist industry in Wales, worth more than 35 times the GDP which renewable electricity could ever realise, and because most of the generation will be wind power, its enormous landscape impact will almost certainly jeopardise tourism.

Of course, BWEA assures us that tourists like the turbines and indeed will swarm to visit wind farms and their eco-centres. But they would say that, wouldn't they? The fact that the Gaia Centre at Delabole went bankrupt, the Swaffham eco-centre encountered serious financial troubles and Cold Northcott visitor centre near Delabole was forced to close, might just be bad luck or rotten management! Interestingly most of the wind farms which are claimed to be tourist attractions are in fact visitor centres in their own right, all in areas where tourists are seeking indoor occupation in bad weather. The Wales Tourist Board summed this up perfectly:

> . . . there will only be a need for a very small number of wind farm visitor centres before this also reaches saturation point. The WTB believe that the case for wind farms as tourist attractions in their own right only has very limited appeal. (Letter to author from WTB, May 2002)

The impact of wind power on tourism may in fact be substantial. In 2003 the Wales Tourist Board concluded from a survey of businesses in mid-Wales that:

> Just over half of the respondents thought wind farms have already and will continue to have an adverse effect on visitors coming to the area.[11]

And we have not even started building a lot of big ones yet!

A survey by VisitScotland (2002) which was effectively conducted "blind" was even more frightening about the impact on tourism, over a quarter of tourists saying they were unlikely to return to a "turbinised" landscape.[12] A similar disturbing conclusion was drawn in the Western Isles where a gigantic development has now fortunately been rejected.[13]

Wind power and jobs

> BWEA, UK's leading renewable energy trade association, welcomed the Prime Minister's endorsement today of the enormous potential of renewable energy to create employment in the UK. (Website, 6 March, 2009)

The reality seems rather different. During construction of Causey Mire wind farm, Caithness, in 2004, a Danish site engineer explained to a visitor that the Bonus turbines had been shipped complete from Denmark. Replying to a question about employment, he commented that no permanent staffing was needed as the day to day operation would be radio controlled from Denmark (a technology well developed in management of offshore wind farms). Maintenance would involve no more than occasional visits to the site by a roving engineer. Cefn Croes, the largest wind farm in Europe, was predicted to need just four full-time employees[14] and at the Bryn Titli wind farm in Wales even the construction site workers were Danish – erecting Danish Bonus turbines in 1994.

At the present time, compared with Denmark, the US, Germany and Spain, the UK has next to no industrial base of large wind turbine manufacture. We make a few blades and towers but essentially the main employment and ownership attributable to any wind farm is overseas.

http://energy.sourceguides.com/businesses/byP/wRP/wRP.shtml

In March 2002, Merfyn Williams, Campaign for the Protection of Rural Wales (CPRW), said (in the *Western Mail*) that the tourism and leisure industry in Wales employs 23,000 people whilst renewable energy (most of which was not then wind power) employs only 275. Thus, though wind farms threaten to destroy jobs in the tourist industry, they create few if any compensating jobs elsewhere.

A recent Spanish study suggests that use of subsidy to drive adoption of renewable electricity generation is expensive and diverts investment from more useful parts of the economy.[15] Wind power costs Spain a huge €1.1 million per job in subsidy and setting minimum prices for renewably generated electricity far above market prices, wastes capital that could be allocated to other sectors. This has resulted in 2.2 jobs being destroyed for every "green job" created.

Assuming that we do need to reduce CO_2-emission, the simple truth is that if the subsidies covertly going into renewables were diverted to other CO_2-conservative projects, thousands of jobs would be created at a stroke, and far more emissions would be saved. For example Connah's Quay 1,400 MW gas-fired CCGT power station, opened in 1996, created or secured 8,000 jobs, and all of the 500 contractors and consultants were based in the UK.

Several gas CCGTs are currently under construction or planned for the UK, for example RWE-npower's 2000 MW station near Pembroke on Milford Haven in Wales. CCGTs emit less than half as much CO_2 per MWh as coal-firing so just one station of this size, displacing an old coal fired station, could potentially save more CO_2 than that of all the UK's wind turbines, which BWEA currently claims as about four million tonnes CO_2 /y in early 2009.

References and notes

1. Letter to Julian and Jane Davis dated April 2008 from Munton & Russel Estate Agents, Spalding, Lincolnshire, confirming that their property had become unsaleable.
2. DBERR *Windpower: 10 myths explained.*
    http://www.berr.gov.uk/whatwedo/energy/sources/renewables/explained/wind/myths/page16060.html Referred to in text as DBERR Myths.

3.   Royal Institution of Chartered Surveyors (2004) *Impact of wind farms on the value of residential property and agricultural land.*

4.   *The Times,* 10 January, 2004.

5.   Remax Estate Agency (2005). *Report on a sample of properties inspected near a proposed wind farm at Esgairwen Fawr.*

6.   *Daily Telegraph* 25 January, 2005.

7.   *Farmers Weekly* 12 January, 2007 *Wind farm noise is driving us out of our house.*

8.   Davis, J & J (2008) evidence to the House of Lords House of Lords Select Committee on Economic Affairs 4th Report of Session 2007–08, *The Economics of Renewable Energy Volume II: Evidence.*

9.   Royal Institution of Chartered Surveyors – Oxford Brookes University (2007) *What is the impact of wind farms on house prices?* Authors Dent, P. & Sims, S.

10. Force 9 website http://force9energy.com/2.html#nine

11. Wales Tourist Board (October 2003) *Investigation into the Potential Impact of Wind Farms on Tourism in Wales. Summary report.*

12. VisitScotland (2003) *Investigation into the Potential Impact of Wind Farms on Tourism in Scotland.*

13. Tourism Operators in North West Lewis (2004).

14. Cefn Croes website http://www.users.globalnet.co.uk/~hills/cc/

15. Calzada Álvarez, G. et al (2009) Study of the effects on employment of public aid to renewable energy sources. Universidad Rey Juan Carlos.

10 Misrepresentation and Manipulation

A truth that's told with bad intent
Beats all the lies you can invent.

(William Blake – *Auguries of Innocence*)

Politics and development of renewable electricity generation

Developments in renewable energy technology have been driven by concerns that greenhouse gases, mainly carbon dioxide (CO_2) from fossil fuel, may cause global warming, and that fossil fuels are approaching exhaustion. Further problems are the environmental, social and political risks of fossil fuels and of nuclear energy.

The growth of the "green" movement during the 1960s and 1970s and on to the present day has strongly influenced the political establishment to the extent that proposed global expenditure on control of the weather is rapidly becoming one of the world's largest budgetary commitments and already commands one of the largest international research expenditures. It was against this backdrop in the late 1990s that the Non-Fossil Fuel Order (NFFO), dating from 1990, was replaced by the Renewables Obligation (RO) which, as we have seen in Chapter 4, presents a huge subsidy to wind power.

The NFFO was emplaced under the provisions of the Electricity Act 1989 by which electricity generation in the UK was privatised. The NFFO was the main policy instrument promoting electricity from Renewable Energy sources in the United Kingdom though its original main aim was to provide finance to the UK nuclear power generators, which were kept in state ownership, not being considered competitive in the private sector. The financial support for these more expensive technologies was provided by a Fossil Fuel Levy on electricity generated from coal, oil or gas. A substantial proportion of the NFFO support went to the nuclear power industry which, in 1990, provided 19% of UK power compared with coal 67%, oil 7%, gas less than one per cent while other renewables, mainly hydroelectricity, gave less than 2%. Wind power did not then exist commercially.

The Non-Fossil Fuel Obligation (NFFO) orders required the electricity Distribution Network Operators in England and Wales to purchase a specified amount of electricity at a set price from the nuclear power and renewable energy sectors. Five such orders were made before the NFFO was replaced by the RO in 2002. However, the last of the existing NFFO orders will continue in effect until it expires in 2018. Since the introduction in 2001 of the New Electricity Trading Arrangements (NETA), electricity suppliers bid for the electricity and ROCs in competitive auctions held by the Non-Fossil Purchasing Agency, with any shortfall in price being funded by the Fossil Fuel Levy. The NFFO has been generating a trading surplus, expected to have reached £500m by 2008.

Despite its almost obsessive pursuit of renewables through the RO, the Government has been criticised for siphoning-off much of the surplus instead of using it to support renewable energy in other ways. In 2005 the House of Commons Committee of Public Accounts wrote "The revenue collected by the Non-Fossil Purchasing Agency . . . now exceeds the amount it pays the contractors . . . The Department [DTI] estimate that the surpluses are likely to accumulate to between £550 million to £1 billion by 2010. The Government has earmarked £60 million of the surpluses to promote the use of renewable energy. The remainder are likely to be paid into the Consolidated Fund and will "benefit the Exchequer". Follow the money!

The introduction of the RO altered the financial structure of the industry by eliminating support from the Fossil Fuel Levy to nuclear power. This was an interesting policy decision considering that even now nuclear power provides 15% of our electricity compared with less than 2% of inferior "quality" supply from wind. Together with wind power and hydroelectricity, nuclear generation is virtually free of CO_2-emission, giving a few grams per kWh compared with almost 900 g CO_2/kWh for coal-fired electricity.

There is no doubt that the RO has worked. In early 2004 the BWEA claimed 648 MW installed capacity of wind in the UK, which had risen to 1,564 MW by April 2006. However this has attracted the critical attention of Parliament. In June 2005 the Commons Committee of Public Accounts remarked that:

> The statement [PPS 22 – see below] increases the chances of hitting the 2010 target, but only by reducing local communities' influence on the planning process.

The PAC report was also deeply critical of the financial arrangement of the RO which it identified as:

> at least four times more expensive than the other means of reducing carbon dioxide currently used in the United Kingdom . . .

One of Prime Minister Blair's last acts in power was to sign up to an EU target for 20% of Europe's total energy to be obtained from renewable sources by 2020, a useful 20/20 sound-bite. The UK currently generates around 2% of its electricity from wind power but to meet the EU's overall energy target the government estimates this will have to increase to 35% to 40% from renewables (mainly wind) in the next 12 years. This is essentially because only electricity has the flexibility of alternatives to fossil fuel. So extreme is this target that a former Chief Scientific Adviser to

Government, Sir David King, has questioned whether a mistake was made and the term "total energy" confused with "electricity".[1]

The recent Climate Change Act goes even further and commits the UK to a targeted 80 per cent reduction in greenhouse gases set for 2050. To facilitate such a reduction the UK will either have to build some 50 GW of extra fossil fuelled power stations for backup, as E.ON UK predicts,[2] or will have to subscribe to the EU proposition of a European supergrid to which we would be linked by a massive set of new interconnections. This has an enormous financial and, more important, political implication. Just as Russia currently has its fingers on the "gas tap" so we would become dependent on Europe leaving the "electricity switch" on. We have also seen that the 4 November, 2006 power failure suggests that even a Europe-wide grid such as UCTE is not immune to the problems caused by wind's uncontrollability.

The EU 20/20 legislation, riding on the back of climate change, may however have a hidden political motivation. Linking into an integrated European Grid to minimise the need for backup power would surely reduce or eliminate the possibility of future secession by the UK.

Reading the foregoing, it is very easy to accept the comment in the ABS *Windpower Report*[3]:

> Wind power has been promoted for politico/environmental reasons and wind developers have benefited from substantial subsidies, leading to exaggerated claims. A reality check is needed.

On 2 March, 2009 it was announced that newly elected President Barack Obama has appointed Jeffrey Immelt, to his new Economic Advisory Board. Immelt is Chairman of the Board of GE which is the fourth largest producer of wind equipment in the world and also the purchaser of the late, unlamented Enron corporation. A day or two later GE's stock was at $6.66. Follow the money!

Development control

By the early years of my life the UK had instituted planning controls which became the envy of the world. The framework for the system was set in the Town and Country Planning Act 1947 which repealed all previous development legislation and was strengthened in 1955 by addition of green belt protection. It was not perfect and powerful property developers quite often managed to obtain permissions against considerable objection but in general the countryside was protected. The system did not alter much after that 1947 Act until the Town and Country Planning Act 1990 and the Planning and Compulsory Purchase Act 2004.

In the early years of the twenty-first century the machinations of the wind power industry quite suddenly made marginal and protected land immensely more valuable than it had been. A hill-farm owner at Blaen Bowi, Carmarthenshire, was reported in the *Tivyside Advertiser* (2002):

> If it wasn't for the windmills I'd have thrown in the towel
> a long time ago.

What landowner, other than a true country lover, could resist the E.ON UK advertisement: "Cash crop – cash in on our renewable energy" which offered landowners earnings of between £5,000 and £8,000 a year for each turbine – much more than the previous cash value of the land they would occupy! Land which is a part of all our aesthetic heritage and a legacy for the future is now threatened by sale to speculators and development on an enormous scale.

The mid-twentieth century planning legislation was meant to guard against exactly this sort of thing but once those "cathedrals" of Chapter 6 became more valuable as crushed road-stone than as vaulting and tracery, legislation came quickly and scandalously to the aid of the wind entrepreneurs. Planning permission was difficult to get or took too long, so let's ride coach and horses through the existing law. The first steps were the Planning Advice Notes – in

England, Planning Policy Statement (PPS 22), in Wales Technical Advice Note 8 (TAN8) and in Scotland National Planning Policy Guideline 6 (NPPG 6). Their advice was typified by:

> Delivering these targets through the planning system is therefore at the core of this TAN.

These targets are installed megawatts capacity of wind power to be achieved by 2010 and 2020. A Freedom of Information enquiry revealed the astounding fact that the Welsh Assembly Government had never calculated the CO_2 mitigation to be expected from the generating capacities proposed in its own planning advice note TAN 8. Landscape-value was barely mentioned other than in the partial exclusion of designated areas such as National Parks!

PPS 22 is less dismissive of landscape and environmental matters but its primary aim also is to introduce "policies designed to promote and encourage, rather than restrict, the development of renewable energy resources". Despite these advisory documents making matters easier for the developers, it was not enough – it never will be.

In England, planning permissions for onshore wind farms of less than 50 MW installed capacity are granted under the Town and Country Planning Act 1990 by Local Planning Authorities (LPAs). Under section 36 of the 1989 Electricity Act projects over 50 MW in capacity were previously determined by DBERR in consultation with the LPA and since 2008 by Department of Energy and Climate Change (DECC). Under the provisions of the 2008 Planning Act, it is expected that by 2010, all Section 36 projects over 50 MW will be determined by The Infrastructure Planning Commission (IPC). The situation in Wales is similar but in Scotland Local Authorities determine all wind turbine proposals under 50MW in capacity while projects exceeding 50 MW are determined by the Scottish Government, in consultation with the LPAs.

The very recent Planning Act 2008 directly affects the wind power scam by adding a duty on councils to take action on climate change in their development plans and also creates an Infrastructure Planning Commission (IPC) as the new authority granting development consent for nationally significant infrastructure projects which include the development of renewables, giving them equal weight to fossil fuels, nuclear power and electricity networks in national policy. We don't yet know how this will affect the rate of wind power development but it seems certain to bode ill for the British landscape and for the secure functioning of the power network.

Misleading or false claims justifying wind power

CO_2 **mitigation by wind power**. It is repeatedly said as a matter of fact that CO_2 emission is offset by wind power sufficiently to alter climate. For example "Harnessing the natural power of the wind is essential to tackle global warming" (Yes2wind).

Commercial wind power arrived in Britain with the opening of the Delabole wind farm, Cornwall, in 1991. The *raison d'être* of the industry even then was the need to reduce CO_2 emission which was believed to be causing global warming. From that time onward substantial misrepresentation was used by the industry to sway the public, to convince politicians and to obtain planning permissions. Very soon the wind industry's publicity campaign was reinforced by government support, soon to become a propaganda campaign epitomised by the DBERR's website *Wind Power: 10 Myths Explained*.

Two claims made in the early years of the industry have resulted in a three to fourfold exaggeration of the real saving of CO_2 emission by wind power, not really corrected until very recently. The first was projection of unrealistically high load factors which ROC Register returns have now revealed. The second concerned the displacement of fossil-fuelled generation. From the outset the industry claimed that coal-fired generation, which has a very high CO_2 emission, would be displaced by wind, but critics of the industry argued that the correct factor could not exceed that of the "grid-mix" of fuels – a weighted average of coal, gas and nuclear. As we saw in Chapter 5, this is half the coal fired factor and there are good arguments for an even smaller number.

In the 1990s neither public nor authorities had any knowledge of wind power, and publicity material rarely mentioned that wind turbines performed on average at about 25% to 30% of their maximum output. Even today the weasel words "up to" are repeatedly used to mislead the public. As I write in December 2008, four wind turbines are being installed by Peel Energy at Liverpool Docks, each of which "will produce up to 2.5 megawatts" according to local press releases. This is a deliberate obfuscation. "Up to" will be a relatively uncommon event, governed by the wind and not by a power station manager as would be the case with thermal generation which can usually provide 100% of capacity on demand.

Sometimes the exaggeration has been more extreme. In the late 1990s Wind Prospect commissioned the Askam Wind Cluster, Old Park Farm, Cumbria, claiming 18 GWh/y as a predicted output from 4.62 MW of installed capacity, which would need a load factor of 44%. The Inspector at a public inquiry into this proposal was sufficiently convinced to write in his letter permitting the development, "The site is a particularly productive one in terms of its average wind velocity." History tells another story. Between 2002 and 2007 the average load factor of Old Park Farm was 24.8% ranging from 18% to 30% so the prediction of electricity generation and CO_2 displacement would have been an exaggeration in excess of almost 1.8 times (Data from CLOWD analysis of ROC Registers). A few more examples are shown in Table 10.1.

If the justification for wind power and its huge adverse impact on landscape is that we must cut CO_2 emission to "tackle climate change" (Yes2Wind) then the above sad story is one of fraudulent selling with a deliberately doubled overestimate of CO_2-saving, coupled with projected electrical outputs which have often been 1.5 times reality or more, hence giving an overall CO_2 displacement of near enough three times reality!

Table 10.1

Station/capacity	Dun Law/16 MW	North Hoyle offshore/60 MW	Cefn Croes/58.5MW
Developer	Renewable Energy Systems (RES)	National Wind Power (now npower)	GE Energy RDC Falck Renewables
Claim	"Will support 14,000 homes". (would need a 47% load factor)	"... meet the demand of 50,000 homes." (would need a 45% load factor)	"... serve about 40,000 households." (would need a 37% load factor)
Actual	5 years' average actual yield 39,433 MWh/y (26% load factor) gives 7704 homes	4 years average 34% load factor gives 37,778 homes	Highest load factor 31% and lowest 25%, of three years. Gives minimum of 27,000 homes
Exaggeration	x 1.8	x 1.3	1.2 to x 1.5
Source	"Powering tomorrow's world", RES (2005)	National Wind Power 2003 website publicity	GE Energy RDC Falck Renewables release

Actual yield and Load factors from CLOWD ROC Register analysis by A. Tubb.
Number of homes calculated from BWEA's 4700 kWh/y/home.

Despite these exaggerations by the industry, the Government has used more believable figures for its calculations.[4] These project a saving of CO_2 emission by renewable power generation, mainly wind, of just 9.2 million tonnes per year by 2010.[5] This is less than three ten-thousandths (0.0003) of global total CO_2 emission and stands no chance of altering atmospheric CO_2 concentration, still less of deflecting climate change.

Thus, whether or not it is an exaggeration that man-made CO_2 emissions will cause harmful global warming, it is impossible for the deployment of wind power in the UK to make the slightest difference. Indeed, the entire CO_2 emission from UK sources is no more than 2% of the global total, so complete depopulation of the British Isles and cessation of all fuel burning would make no more than a 2% difference to world emission. Even the most ambitious wind power target for 2020 will not exceed a mitigation of more than 0.2% of global emission. As I have written elsewhere (with apologies to Voltaire's supposed remark on God), "If global warming did not exist it would be necessary for the wind power industry to invent it".[6]

Denmark is a wind power showcase. Supporters of wind power chant a mantra that Denmark proves that wind power works. BWEA says it "now gets 20% of its electricity from wind turbines . . ."[7] This is a cynically deliberate confusion of production with consumption. The 20% is of production and applies only to West Denmark which has most of the wind turbines. For the whole country the percentage is c.13% from wind.

More to the point, much of this electricity has perforce been exported to adjacent countries because it was produced when it is not needed. In some years over four fifths of the annual production has been exported, sometimes at zero income, thus costing the Danish public about DKK 1 billion (roughly £100 million) per year though more recent estimates put annual losses at or above DKK 1.5 billion.[8]

In the words of an electrical engineer based in Denmark: "I think the right number for wind power consumption in West Denmark would be 7-8% during 2007, an exceptionally wet and windy year" (pers comm, 9 October, 2008). This is hardly a good advertisement in a country with the most installed wind power per head of any in the world, and a leading manufacturer of wind turbines. US physicist Howard Hayden rightly remarked some years ago:

The little country Denmark has made a name in recent years with their wind turbines. No, they don't produce much electricity, they sell them to suckers!.

Denmark can support a high penetration of wind power because it fortuitously had large capacity interlinks to Norway, Sweden and Germany before substantial wind power was developed. Norway is virtually 100% hydroelectric and Sweden is half hydro- and half nuclear so these exports not only cost Denmark dearly but often displace little additional CO_2 emission as they are balanced by instantly controllable hydro-.

The magnitude of the daily export is directly proportional to the amount of wind power generated, for example Sharman[9] shows data from Eltra, the West Danish Transmission Company, for June 2003 in which the graphs of wind generation and net international power exchange are virtually mirror images of each other – a remarkably high level of correlation. The 2003 annual report of Eltra "suggests an export figure of 84% of total wind production to these countries [Norway, Sweden and Germany] in 2003 . . ."[10]

Rather have wind than nuclear. Another mantra repetition is that wind turbines are preferable to nuclear power: "They are also vital in ending the threat of nuclear power . . ." (Yes2Wind). This is untruthful as it is not possible for wind power, however much is installed, to displace nuclear power. The reason for this is that our present fleet of nuclear stations cannot be ramped up and down and are operated at continuous peak output, providing unvarying baseload generation. It is quite impossible for wind to do this, as its availability is at the mercy of wind. If as Government has suggested, a new nuclear programme is started with modern Pressurized Water Reactors such as the AREVA EPR, they will also be best-suited to baseload provision but will also allow load-following operation. Wind power cannot load follow either as, again, it may not be available. It was for these reasons amongst others, that the Sustainable Development Commission concluded in 2005 that "it would be unrealistic to assume that wind energy would displace any nuclear capacity . . ."[4]

Modern wind turbines are quiet. Noise has become a more sensitive issue as turbines are built ever-closer to communities and it needs little more than a glance at the BWEA website's comments on noise and comparison of this with reality to expose deliberate misrepresentation. BWEA's website says:

> It should be emphasised that typical noise levels are so low for a carefully considered site that they would normally be drowned out by a nearby stream or by a moderate breeze in nearby trees and hedgerows.

We saw in Chapter 7 that there are now numerous cases of lives being seriously disrupted by turbine noise, some planning applications have been withdrawn or rejected on the grounds of noise and the government system of assessing wind power noise is not fit for purpose.

The saga of the Davis family, recounted in Chapters 7 and 9, is a salutary example. Originally sufficiently supportive of wind power not to object to its construction, they have been driven from their home, now unsellable, by noise from Deeping St Nicholas wind farm near Spalding, Lincolnshire. Julian and Jane Davis' story is perhaps an extreme one but they are far from alone, with reports from across the world of developers buying-out victims of their machines rather than face increasingly adverse publicity (Chapter 7).

Many homes can be supported. BWEA currently estimates that 1,839,538 UK homes are "supported" by wind power (February 09) whilst Shell claimed that: "The 1,000 MW London Array would . . . be able to generate enough electricity to cater for the power needs of a quarter of London homes." I concur with US physicist Howard Hayden, author of *The Solar Fraud*, who described such claims as "misleading garbage". The spurious accuracy of the BWEA figure also raises some suspicion about the competence of the calculation!

From the consumers' point of view an electricity system must deliver power (kW) whenever a switch is flicked and here we have the misrepresentation. To remain live, the switch must always be connected to mains electricity and yet the average Jo in the street would interpret wind "supporting" a home as provision of a continuous supply. Policy makers and environmentalists constantly refer to energy delivered over a time period (MWh or kWh), whether or not it is securely available at a specified time. It is thus a half-truth used as a lie that the power needs of the homes are met. Energy is delivered by wind power only when available, and power would repeatedly be cut off or reduced if the wind supply operated without backup generation, incurring carbon costs and enormous financial implications.

Wind power provides a local supply. Wind farm developments have been repeatedly justified by claims concerning local or targeted use of the power. In the early days of the North Hoyle Offshore Wind Farm, npower had this to say:

> An exciting new green electricity product called Juice was launched in Rhyl, North Wales on 1 August, 2001 by npower, the national energy supplier and Greenpeace. This project, the first of its kind between Greenpeace and an energy company provides an opportunity for domestic customers to purchase clean electricity from the North Hoyle Offshore Wind Farm.

More recently npower claimed it had contracted with Marks & Spencer to provide 2.7 TWh per year of renewable electricity to supply M&S' stores. However the ROC registers show that N. Hoyle has an annual generation near 0.2 TWh, less than a tenth of the energy promised to M&S. How could npower possibly have claimed cleverly to separate electricity from N. Hoyle to supply identified customers? The claim is still effectively made as their 2009 website describes the electricity as "from a renewable energy source, primarily . . . North Hoyle".

Electricity from any source feeds into either the distribution networks or into the high voltage Grid. Because the energy travels at nearly the speed of light it will manage the length of the British Isles in a three hundredth of a second, taking such routes in the network as to satisfy instantaneous demand. It is an utter nonsense, a travesty of physics, to speak of electricity from a cluster of wind turbines being "used" by a nearby village! This would only be true if they were connected to each home by a "green" cable, independently of the mains supply. In reality that nearby village uses the same "dirty" mix of fossil fuel and nuclear that supplies me in west Wales, my daughter in London and my wife's family in Scotland – all with instantaneous access to the Grid which is effectively a tiny pool with huge inputs and outputs.

Thus, in 2008 we all plugged-in to gas, coal, nuclear and wind in the proportions 34%, 43%, 15% and less than 2%, with a total of 92% of even the greenest tariff's supply coming from "smoky black" or "glowing red" sources which are no different from the composition of my own standard tariff with the SWALEC subsidiary of S&SE!

It is however open to all of us to choose our electricity supplier and to pay their prevailing unit-rate. So far as the author is aware there never has been or will be a commercial arrangement to cable-connect wind electricity directly to a home which is in reach of "mains" electricity. To avoid ASA actions for false claims a clever choice of words has been forced upon the green-scheme suppliers. There are two possibilities – firstly for example npower says:

> . . . for every unit of electricity they [customers] use, npower feeds the same amount to the electricity network from a renewable energy source.

Secondly, green fund customers donate money into a fund that supports new renewable capacity or other related initiatives. But, as all ordinary consumers are already paying a premium on their bills to support the RO, and as there are so many more of them, one wonders just what the green tariff supplier is actually offering and whether "green" is simply a cynical marketing ploy?

Not many turbines are needed. BWEA's "Top myths about wind power" denies the suggestion that "Tens of thousands of wind turbines will be cluttering the British countryside". It correctly claims, "3,500 additional modern wind turbines will be needed to deliver 8% of the UK's electricity by 2010, roughly 2,000 onshore and 1,500 offshore." As it says, the 3,500 turbines are additional thus bringing the total to 5,500 but the Government wants 20% by 2020 – thus 11,000. Worse – to reach the EU's target of 20% of ALL energy by 2020 would require 40% of electricity to come from renewables because such large savings in other sectors are impossible. That would double the number to over 20,000 turbines – thus tens of thousands seems a reasonable forecast as experience says the numbers will grow.

Rural, green and powerful? During the development of the oil industry in the early 1900s a cluster of storage tanks became known as a "tank farm". This represented the industry as more "rural" than the reality; today we would say "greener" and now we have wind "farms" rather than wind power stations. Likewise the name "wind turbine" is an exercise in spin. Ask any engineer to describe a "turbine" and two common factors emerge. A turbine is a complex multi-bladed device operating within a shroud and gives enormous power for its size. Wind turbines were formerly known as "aerogenerators", a term still used by a few manufacturers. When there is enough wind, they have a power output of just two or three megawatts, compared with the hundreds of megawatts from a power station steam turbine. The inappropriate name successfully misleads, and few people realise that it needs a thousand or two wind turbines to match the annual output of a fossil fuelled power station.

Communities will be given a financial stake. "Community benefits" (aka bribes) are universally offered by wind developers. An example is the current planning application for Mynydd-y-Gwair wind farm in S. Wales for which nPower published a flier at least two years before the application was lodged. It says:

> . . . We are keen to investigate opportunities for community benefit. The fund is likely to be in the region of between £50,000 and £70,000 per year over the lifetime of the project . . .

DBERR (the former DTI) has issued a report entitled *Delivering Community Benefits from Wind Energy Development: A Toolkit*. This strongly makes the point that:

> There is a strict principle in the planning systems in all parts of the UK that a decision about a particular planning proposal should be based on planning issues . . . To put it simply, planning permission can not be "bought".

The Welsh TAN 8 planning document says much the same:

> . . . the important point here is that, as such offers are not necessary for the development to proceed, **they must not impact upon the decision-making process**. [emboldening as in original] (Annex B. 1.3) [and] It must be clear that the provision of benefits is on a purely voluntary basis with no connection to the planning application process. (Annex B. 2.4)

Most such offers have been bandied about in the local press and in developers fliers during the consultation period prior to planning. How can this **not** influence the planning process? How many such permissions have been helped through by such offers and I ask: "Are the approvals legal if offers have been previously publicised?"

Wind power will improve security of energy supply. This might be true in the broad sense that wind power can be harvested in the UK whereas much fossil fuel is imported, some from politically unstable and problematic sources. Unfortunately wind is so unpredictably intermittent that its deployment in any quantity which will significantly affect carbon emission, will either introduce serious unreliability to the power system or will demand a huge investment in extra thermal generating capacity so negating the intention. As Lord Vallance said in opening the 2009 House of Lords Debate on the economics of renewable:

> reserve plant is indispensable as little electricity can be stored. It will have to be very substantial indeed as the capacity credit of wind turbines – that is, the share of their output capacity which can be relied upon – is very low.[11]

Eight or nine out of ten people want wind power.

> Opinion surveys regularly show that just over eight out of ten people are in favour of wind energy, and less than one in ten (around 5%) are against it. BWEA FAQs.

Chapter 6 revealed that the truth is very different from this if we look at the real world of planning applications and polls, where the outcome is not steered by clever use of the introductory question "Do you support renewable energy?" The explosive response to the Isle of Lewis planning application far from being 85% support was indeed 99.5% opposition! This was extreme, and most such statistics suggest that there is hard-core support for wind power from perhaps a quarter of the population.

Both camps are deeply committed to their feelings and attempts by developers to steamroller the opposition have been very damaging to local communities, setting neighbour against neighbour and former friends at loggerheads. The Davis family, mentioned above, have summed this up well in their evidence to the House of Lords,[12] for example a comment on a Norfolk application:

> Marshland St James Norfolk: there has been considerable animosity ever since the wind farm was first mooted. This has now divided the whole village. Unusually – in our experience – this is the only village where there has been criminal activity, damage to property, vandalism, arson attacks, and tragically a suicide. An internet search will give you much of the detail . . .

Many more examples abound – for example in South Wales at a proposed wind farm several wind monitoring masts have been mysteriously destroyed. Coercion and intimidation are not one-sided: in 2002 the BWEA posted on its website a list of names, including the author's, accompanied by the old street-threat: "We know where you live" (*Western Mail*, 30 Sept, 2000). No one can support such illegal actions but it does reveal the strength of feeling which will increase as the attack on democracy grows.

References and notes

1. UK's top boffin: Renewables targets were "a mistake". *The Register*, 4 September, 2008.
2. E.ON UK evidence to the House of Lords. House of Lords Select Committee on Economic Affairs 4th Report of Session 2007–08 The Economics of Renewable Energy Volume II: Evidence [90% or more of intermittent renewable generation such as wind will need to be backed up by more flexible fossil-fired capacity to help ensure that sufficient generating capacity is available at winter peak. Consideration has to be given to how investment in that additional conventional plant is to be incentivised and rewarded, when some of it may only run on an

infrequent basis.] See also Business Green (04 Jun, 2008) "The company [E.ON] said the UK would require 50GW of renewable energy to meet the EU target, but that would require up to 45GW of backup capacity from coal and gas-fired plants . . ."

3. ABS Energy Research (2006) ABS *Windpower Report*.

4. Sustainable Development Commission (2005) *Windpower in the UK* (November 2005 corrected reprint).

5. (a) DBERR *Wind Power: 10 Myths Explained* quotes a 2010 figure of 2.5 Mt carbon/year to be saved by renewable electricity generation [mainly wind]. This is equivalent to 9.2 Mt CO_2. (b) Department of Energy and Climate Change (2008) *UK Climate Change Sustainable Development Indicator: 2007 Greenhouse Gas Emissions, Final Figures.* Gives 38 billion tonnes CO_2 total global emission p.a. of human origin – by ratio the UK renewable electricity target saving is 0.00024 – just over two ten-thousandths).

6. Etherington, J.R. *The Wind Monster* (2005).

7. BWEA http://www.bwea.com/energy/europe.html

8. World Nuclear Association, 2007 *Nuclear energy in Denmark*. http://www.world-nuclear.org/info/inf99.html

9. Sharman, H (2005) Incoteco (Denmark). Presentation: Planning for Intermittency: The Importance of Evidence from Germany and Denmark. UK ERC Workshop –Imperial College. [Wind output is nearly always mirrored by almost equal net exports from Denmark (slide for June 2003). The massive E.ON wind power system in N. Germany is also strongly interconnected to eight adjacent power systems.]

10. White, D. (July 2004) Danish Wind: Too Good to be True? *The Utilities Journal* pp 37-39.

11. *Hansard* (24 Feb. 2009) House of Lords. *Debate: Report of the Economic Affairs Committee on The Economics of Renewable Energy.*

12. Davis, J & J (2008) evidence to the House of Lords. House of Lords Select Committee on Economic Affairs 4th Report of Session 2007–08 *The Economics of Renewable Energy Volume II: Evidence.*

11 Climate change and Kyoto – Is it all necessary?

There is no opinion, however absurd, which men will not readily embrace as soon as they can be brought to the conviction that it is generally adopted. (Arthur Schopenhauer)

Whether the post-Kyoto control of carbon dioxide and other greenhouse gases is necessary to tackle climate change is still a matter of considerable dissent – despite political projection of consensus that "the debate is over". Whatever the outcome of the controversy, it is quite obvious from the foregoing chapters that wind power could make little or no contribution in any circumstances. Even if one were to accept the tenets of a simple, one-factor CO_2-driven model of climatic warming it can be shown that wind power is not able to provide a significant or cost effective means of displacing CO_2 emission, or limiting fossil fuel consumption sufficiently to alter climate.

British windmills cannot significantly affect global warming so why write about it in a book on wind power? The decision is forced upon me by the repeated governmental support for wind power in the name of controlling the weather. Ed Miliband, the Minister for Climate Change, for example said:

> It is socially unacceptable to be against wind turbines . . .
> (Press statement on viewing *The Age of Stupid*)

There is no dispute that climate has changed on the scale of centuries, mostly long before man had any influence, and it will continue to do so, driven by natural processes, though within surprisingly narrow limits. It is also not disputed that man-made climate change may be caused by accidental alteration of atmospheric composition and its natural greenhouse effect. What is in dispute is the amount of warming which can be caused by a specified increase in a greenhouse gas.

The natural greenhouse effect occurs because the atmosphere is largely transparent to solar radiation, which warms the earth, but is partly opaque to the loss of infrared radiation which keeps earth cool. It may be visualised as a one-way door for heat, resulting in a warmer earth. The natural greenhouse maintains a temperature high enough for life to exist but it is also suggested that the man-made contribution to greenhouse activity may recently be causing it to become too hot for comfort.

Before we can understand the control and maintenance of earth's temperature in the narrow limits which supports life we need to ask "What is 'global warming'?" (or as it has been renamed for strategic reasons, "climate change", a catch-all if there ever was!). It is often implicitly man-made and a threat to life, even though the historical past has seen relatively enormous climatic shifts such as the Roman Warm Period and the Medieval Warm Period and, a little later the Little Ice Age, long before man measurably influenced the atmosphere with fossil fuel CO_2 and other greenhouse gases (GHGs).

A simplistic answer requires a little bit of physics which I will attempt to explain without too many numbers. For simplicity, let's assume the earth is a globe with a very thin skin of atmosphere at the top of which is an imaginary "transparent ceiling" through which no heat can travel by convection or conduction. This barrier approximately models reality as the only significant energy exchanges between sun, earth and the cosmos are radiation at wavelengths ranging from long-wave infrared, through the visible down into the ultraviolet and short-wave X-ray and gamma-ray wavelengths. There is some transfer of energy by gravitation, causing tidal friction heating, but so small in quantity that it can be neglected in relation to global temperature. Below the ceiling, convection of heat and water plays the major part in creating weather and its long term average, climate. Evaporation of water and its precipitation transport huge amounts of energy vertically into the troposphere (lower atmosphere) and horizontally from low to high latitudes.

Energy from the sun reaches us as short-wave radiation (a mixture of visible light, ultraviolet and infrared). The atmosphere and earth's surface absorb much of this radiation, the balance being reflected back to the cosmos mostly from cloud tops.

This absorption of radiant energy by the sunward hemisphere warms earth's surface and atmosphere, and without a balancing process earth would rapidly heat up to a lethal temperature. The balance is provided by loss of long-wave infrared radiation (radiant heat). All bodies warmer than absolute zero (zero Kelvin or minus 273°C) radiate energy – visible light or shortwave infrared if they are very hot like the sun, or long-wave thermal infrared from cooler bodies such as the planets. There is in fact a continuum of decreasing wavelength of emission as temperature of the emitting body falls and it is also the case that a very hot body radiates enormously more energy per unit of surface area, than a cool one. Furthermore, all bodies exposed to radiant energy of any wavelength, absorb a part and reflect the remainder.

Earth's average temperature (if there is such a thing on so diverse a planet!) is defined by just three energy exchanges through that imaginary transparent lid to the atmosphere.

a. "Downward" solar short-wave visible and invisible "sunlight" passing freely through the lid. Global average 342 watt per m^2 (W/m^2).

b. "Upward" reflection of part of that income back to space, largely by cloud cover and some by reflection from the surface. Global average 107 W/m^2.

c. "Upward" loss of long-wave infrared radiation from surface and atmosphere to space. Global average 235 W/m^2.

If solar income (a) is constant, which it effectively is as an annual average, and if cloud cover and surface reflectivity (albedo) remained constant, so upward reflection of short-wave energy (b) will be constant. To balance the budget the net upward loss of long-wave (c) must equal the difference between income and reflection of the short-wave solar energy (a - b) thus (342 -107) - 235 = 0 (American Meteorological Society estimates). The zero of this balanced budget implies that earth is at a constant temperature – there being no residual energy to warm it or loss of energy to cool it. In the real world each of the three radiant components may change and alter the equilibrium temperature, as we shall see.

It is a matter of geological history that these three processes have kept surface temperature in the very narrow range to preserve the molecular structure of life for over 3.5 billion years. At present it averages about 15°C. Living processes cannot continue much below 0°C and above about 60°C to 70°C almost all organisms die because their proteins and nucleic acids are destroyed. That I am here to write this, and you are reading it at this moment in geological time, is of great significance to the controversy about regulation of earth's surface temperature and the "global warming" debate. It implies that whatever has happened in the past has not been able to trigger run-away warming or cooling, otherwise all our shared inheritance of genetic material would have been snuffed out long before it had legs!

How does the greenhouse effect and consequent global warming relate to the atmosphere and its composition beneath that imaginary transparent ceiling? If the constituents of the atmosphere allow short-wave solar radiation in, this will cause warming of the surface and lower atmosphere. The warmed molecules will consequently emit long-wave infrared radiation. If the atmosphere absorbs this radiation it will prevent loss of energy to the cosmos and earth and lower atmosphere would grow warmer. This process was historically named the "greenhouse effect", and gases in the atmosphere which are transparent to short wave but blanket long wave radiation are "greenhouse gases". We have no space here to explore the argument about the appropriateness of the "greenhouse" simile – suffice to say it is a simplification which is at least 200 years old[1] and serves well in an elementary explanation. That's what simplifications are for.

Speculation on the warming effect of CO_2 on global climate dates back to the nineteenth century but it was only in the 1950s that systematic attempts to monitor air CO_2 concentration began. C.D. Keeling's continuous measurements of carbon dioxide in the atmosphere started in 1958 and quickly established that it was rising fast.[2] The time-course is often now referred to as the "Keeling Curve".[3] Other researchers soon took an interest in how the level of CO_2 had changed in the past and how it was influenced by chemical and biological forces. Initially this seemed of no practical significance, and unlikely to receive research funding. However through the '70s and '80s a few workers vociferously claimed that the gas plays a crucial role in climate change, and that the rising level could seriously affect our future.

These claims led to the establishment of the Intergovernmental Panel on Climate Change (IPCC) in 1988 by the World Meteorological Organization (WMO) and the United Nations Environment Programme (UNEP), two organizations of the United Nations. The IPCC does not carry out research, nor does it monitor climate but publishes special reports relevant to the implementation of the UN Framework Convention on Climate Change, adoption of which led eventually to the Kyoto Protocol. By the time of the 1995 Second Assessment Report the IPCC confidently claimed, "The balance of evidence suggests a discernible human influence on global climate".

The United Nations Conference on Environment and Development, commonly known as the Rio Summit, which was held in June 1992 had its foundation partly in the IPCC's work. More than 100 national leaders signed the Convention on Climate Change and adopted Agenda 21, a plan for achieving sustainable development in the twenty-first century. This was a further step toward the Kyoto Protocol on global warming which was adopted in 1997, came into force in 2005 and now in 2009 has 183 ratifying signatories.

The agreement was intended to reduce global emissions of carbon dioxide and other minor GHGs to 1990 levels or below during the period 2008-2012. Crucially, the protocol was based on the assumption that carbon dioxide was the main factor in driving global warming and indeed the only quantitative annex to the summary of actions taken in 1997, was a list of countries, their CO_2 emissions and percentage contribution to emission of the gas.[4] However, the atmospheric concentration of CO_2 continued to rise at about the same rate it did before Kyoto, at a steady 1-2 parts per million by volume (ppmv) per year and until the 2000s, global average temperature rose with it, albeit not so steadily. "Global warming" became a household word and vested interests targeted governments and academia with demands to "do something".

Up to this point, contributors to the warming debate on either side would not be likely to argue too much with this account. It is a matter of fact that air concentration of CO_2 has been increasing at one to two ppmv per year at least from the 1950s and carbon isotope studies suggest that much of the increment has come from fossil fuel. All physicists would accept that long wave absorption by this extra CO_2 will cause some warming of the troposphere and surface, but the magnitude of radiative forcing and consequent temperature rise is in dispute. It is also correct that a generalised warming has continued sporadically since the late 1800s – before man could have had much influence. It accounts for much of the total recent warming and is usually interpreted as emergence from the cold of the Little Ice Age. There is controversy about the impact of man-made CO_2 in the later years of the twentieth century and to what extent it has driven additional warming, in particular because warming has now slowed or even reversed for a decade.

These recent events can be seen in the global temperature record, compiled by the UK Meteorological Office's Hadley Centre for Climate Prediction and Research, which starts in 1850. This presents the temperature change as an anomaly – expressed as difference from the average of 1961-90.[5]

During the period 1850-1900 the anomaly oscillated between minus 0.4°C up to minus 0.2°C. Shortly after the turn of the century a steady increase took the anomaly to + 0.1°C by 1940. The temperature then dropped sharply back to an average anomaly of about minus 0.2°C, maintained until the late 1970s when the "modern warming" began as a continuous uniform increase lasting for some 30 years and taking the anomaly to about +0.5°C, reaching a record high in 1998. This 1998 record coincided with and was amplified by an El Niño event and even now ten years later has never been exceeded.

If, and only if, a starting point is chosen at the commencement of one of these two 30 to 40 year warmings, for example 1970-2000, the cumulative temperature rise is highly correlated with the CO_2 concentration. However an alternative choice such as 1940-1980 shows virtually zero correlation between CO_2 and temperature (assuming CO_2 concentration can be extrapolated into the past as the IPCC does).

After the 1998 record high, global temperature-change dropped back in line with its pre-El Niño course but from 2002 the evidence suggests that the 30-year "modern warming" has stopped and latterly has become a four-year cooling. It is far too soon to draw conclusions about climate change but is of huge significance that since 1998 there has been no correlation between the inexorably rising CO_2 concentration and global temperature.

The protagonists of global warming explain this recent cessation of temperature-rise but continuing CO_2 increase by claiming that other natural processes have masked the ongoing warming. This may be so, but it also suggests that the earlier warming may have been part of a natural oscillation. As the IPCC's and other computer models of climate failed to predict this cessation of warming it means that at least one unknown parameter is missing from the modelling. What is it? and what else is missing?

It is not credible that the virtual-world output of the models can be reliably used to make policy decisions.

Neither is this the only failure of prediction by the models. Their projections suggested that the troposphere should show more warming than the surface but in fact its temperature has been virtually unchanged since 1979 if El Niños and volcanic eruptions are taken into account.[6] The inability of models to retrospectively explain events in the more distant past compounds doubts whether huge financial commitments should be gambled on their future output.

Temperature in the past

It is not only in recent history that CO_2 appears to have no effect as a warming gas. The geological past has seen great changes in atmospheric CO_2 concentration, global temperature, cloud cover and sea level. In the distant past CO_2 has been enormously higher than the present level – it was over ten times the modern concentration in the early Palaeozoic era, including glacial periods during the Ordovician period (490 to 443 Ma). Prior to this, with even higher CO_2 our planet had experienced several major glacial periods (600-700 Ma) when the entire Earth was ice-covered for long periods.[7] The coexistence of high CO_2 concentration and glaciation, not to mention spontaneous recovery from what could have become run-away freezing, suggests that CO_2 alone simply cannot be the sole driver of climatic temperature change.

During the present Quaternary Period, covering the past 2 million or so years, there has been a cyclic repetition of 30 to 40 warm and cold events – the coldest becoming full glaciations. We know from ice-core sampling in Antarctica and Greenland that CO_2 and methane (CH_4) rose and fell in concentration, correlated with the temperature changes but lagging a few hundred years after them.[8] There could of course have been no man-made effect on CO_2 concentration during any of these cyclic oscillations or the changes of temperature in deeper geological time.

We live in a late-interglacial period and because of cyclic recurrence, almost for certain the cycle will repeat itself. The temperatures at our latitude became sub-tropical in the last interglacial and the sea rose to several metres above the present level. For the future of mankind, it is important that we recognise that this will happen and as it is unlikely that human intervention could safely deflect the process, we need to conserve resources to adapt to these changes as they develop. "The Age of Stupid" will almost certainly prove to be the time when we threw away essential resources in symbolic acts akin to those Bronze Age sacrificial-offerings intended to ensure that the sun would continue to rise.

The warming process during the current interglacial is already well documented. Temperature has been rising in sporadic fashion since the maximum of the last glaciation (c.18,000 years ago), faster during the final de-glaciation (ended c.10,000 years ago) but it has continued sporadically ever since though more slowly in the past 2,000-3,000 years. At the height of the last glaciations about 18,000 BP [Before Present], sea level was about 100 m below the present level consequent on land-locking of ice and thermal contraction of ocean water, aided and abetted by alterations of land level caused by the weight of ice.

During the post-glacial warming there have been "hiccups" – the sudden re-freezing of the Younger Dryas was the most prominent and plunged earth back into cold from 15,000 BP to 13,000 BP with dramatic cooling and then a warming of several °C within a century or less, all without the carbon footprint of man. Several smaller changes are evidenced by many paleoclimatic proxies or are historically recorded; thus we have the Bronze Age and Roman Warm Periods, the Medieval Warm Period and the Little Ice Age, the harsh winters of which to this day give us our Dickensian Christmas card visions of snows and cosy cottage lamps.

None of these great changes in the past can be attributed to man-made CO_2. It is possible that the present human contribution to CO_2 increase may speed the warming process but before embarking on hugely expensive policy decisions, the proponents of warming must explain how CO_2 and CH_4 increased previously without human intervention and of course why they followed rather than preceded temperature change (see below). More crucially, how did rising or falling CO_2 concentration switch as the climate cooled or warmed into the succeeding glacial and interglacial periods? What physical process switches between warming and cooling in the absence of human interference? We do not know – and what is fast becoming the world's biggest ever commercial enterprise will be based upon total ignorance, indeed the true age of the stupid.

Consensus is crumbling

As a former peer reviewer and editor of an international journal, I am shocked by the discussion-stopper from politicians and journalists (even the occasional inexplicable scientist) that "debate on climate-change is over" – that there is "consensus". This is simply not true nor how science works. It is certainly not how the incredibly complex science of climatology works as IPCC itself recorded – probably now to its own embarrassment.

> We are dealing with a coupled non-linear chaotic system, and therefore the prediction of a specific future climate state is not possible.[9]

The future projections of the IPCC are essentially based on mathematical modelling and it is significant that the IPCC calls the models and outputs "storylines" each of which belong to scenario families. The climate models calculate the consequences of increasing atmospheric GHG concentrations and an illustrative scenario was chosen for each of six scenario groups which were refined down from 40 original groups. The 2002 Special Emissions report notes that no judgment is offered as to preference for any of the scenarios:

> [The scenarios] are not assigned probabilities of occurrence, neither must they be interpreted as policy recommendations.[10]

Politicians and the media have deliberately disregarded this warning against misuse and inevitably represent the worst-case scenarios of greatest change. As a result of this disregard, the world is now committed to the greatest expenditures it is likely to make, but with no guarantee that any specific outcome will be achieved. The computer generated futures are a virtual reality and, lacking numbers and sometimes signs for important parameters such as reflection of energy income by clouds, cannot be relied on to be more accurate than tomorrow's weather forecast.

The impression which has been projected to the media and the public by the IPCC is very simple: that CO_2-emission is increasing at an exponential rate, that atmospheric concentration will follow that increase and because it is a greenhouse gas global temperature will rise. Lo and behold, if we start in 1970 and stop in 2000 as we saw above – we have demonstrable global warming and thus hysteria has erupted.

However if we move forward into the last decade or backward in history by say 1,000 years or further through geological time, there is no evidence for CO_2-driven warming (or cooling for that matter). During the past decade CO_2 has risen uniformly but there has been no overall temperature rise. Likewise in the period 1940 to 1970 there was no correlation between increasing CO_2 and temperature.

Looking further back the most remarkable failure of CO_2 warming theory is derived from the late Quaternary ice core record of temperature, CO_2 and methane, especially those from the Vostok Antarctic base where there is a continuous record covering 420,000 years and several glacial-inter glacial cycles.[11] In his film, An Inconvenient Truth, Mr Gore triumphantly said that when CO_2 goes up and down, so does temperature. Unfortunately for this "proof" that CO_2 is the driver, higher resolution analyses of the cores revealed that it is temperature change which precedes the dissolved gases by between 200 and 1,000 years for the last three deglaciations.

Thus the assumption that CO_2 controls climatic warmth appears to be a good story spoiled by ugly facts. That temperature moves first is falsification of the CO_2 driver hypothesis – CO_2 patently cannot be the initial driver of temperature change. It is most likely that temperature is driving evolution of CO_2 by the warming of seawater, which reduces the solubility of the gas.

CO_2 concentration is increasing a lot; how can it not cause warming?

One answer lies in feedback. A refrigerator does not get too cold or too warm because it has a thermostat which senses temperature and imposes a negative feedback. When too warm it cools and when too cold it switches off and warms slightly. Many natural systems, physical or biological, have feedback mechanisms. Negative ones maintain stability whilst positive ones promote runaway change.

By far the most important natural GHG is water vapour which can also change to liquid water (cloud) in the atmosphere with effect on both incoming solar radiation which it reflects, and upward long-wave radiation, which it absorbs. As a global average, water vapour and cloud contribute more than three-quarters of the natural "greenhouse" which makes earth habitable rather than a frozen "snowball". The reflection of short-wave income by cloud reduces average solar energy input by about 20% but both vapour and cloud also reduce cooling by blanketing long wave infrared loss.

Warm air can contain much more water vapour than cold air so any warming process will cause evaporation of water into the lower atmosphere then, as it is transported by atmospheric convective processes, it may condense as cloud. Low level cloud in particular imposes a negative feedback on warming by reflecting solar income, whilst high altitude cirrus cloud may add more blanketing and act as a positive feedback to warming.

Long before I encountered the problems of wind power discussed in this book, I taught undergraduate biologists elementary environmental physics which included outlines of earth's energy balance and the radiant energy budget of ecological systems as it relates to the water cycle and carbon fixation by photosynthesis.

At that time (1975) I wrote:

> [The] energy budget of the earth's surface may be altered by the "greenhouse effect"; the trapping of long wave black-body re-radiation of energy, from the earth's surface, into space. This effect is due to the transparency of CO_2 to the shortwave income from the sun and its opacity to the much longer wave, low temperature re-radiation. The obvious consequence would be an increase in atmospheric temperature but further alterations such as an increase in global cloud cover might also be expected to have a homeostatic effect.[12]

Looking back over 34 years this seems a bit naive, but one thing which remains true is that alterations to the water cycle and cloud cover could impose a negative feedback, so providing self-regulation (homeostasis) of temperature. This would prevent CO_2 or other greenhouse gases from driving temperature inexorably upward or downward as they change in concentration. The UN's Intergovernmental Panel on Climate Change (IPCC) has recognised this possibility. For example the 2001 3rd Assessment Report listed amongst "Key Uncertainties":

> Factors associated with model projections, in particular . . . climate forcing, and feedback processes especially those involving water vapor, clouds, and aerosols.[13]

The 2007 4th Assessment Report remained remarkably vague about water despite the fact that no mathematical model can give a useful predictive simulation if any key parameter cannot be quantified. It said:

Cloud feedbacks remain the largest source of uncertainty.[14]

An earlier IPCC report had expressed not only doubt about the magnitude of the feedback from the water cycle but also admitted its sign was not known. Whether water provides a positive or a negative signal is crucial to predictive modelling and if the value is simply guessed at, the output of the model is equivalently guesswork – "garbage in – garbage out" in the words of wise modellers. As I said above – we do not know.

In addition to the low-level cloud reflective feedback it is now apparent that infrared blanketing by high altitude cirrus cloud may vary in response to surface temperature. In 2001 Lindzen *et al.* suggested that high cirrus cloud over the tropical Pacific dissipated as the sea surface warmed, thus opening an "iris" for escape of long wave infrared.[15] Further support has come from Spencer's recent work at the University of Alabama. If this mechanism is widespread, and operates on global warming, "it would reduce estimates of future warming by over 75 per cent".[16]

A second reason why increasing CO_2 may not drive substantial warming is that the "blanketing" effect is logarithmically related to concentration – sequential equal increments of CO_2 give progressively less warming. If we look at the escape of long wave radiation through the atmospheric lid, it is as if there are a number of windows to the cosmos (corresponding to wavelengths of radiant absorption by CO_2). If there were no CO_2, some of the windows would still be curtained as water vapour and cloud has already blocked them. The first increment of CO_2 pulls a thin curtain over the remaining windows so less energy spills out and the planet warms. The next thin curtain has less effect, and very soon, extra curtains make no significant difference to blocking radiant energy.

The net effect of doubling CO_2 concentration can be expressed as the imbalance of radiant energy passing the lid – often referred to as a "forcing factor" expressed in W/m^2. If a net downward energy flux results, this is a positive forcing factor and, via the Stefan-Boltzmann relationship, can also be converted to a predicted surface warming and new higher equilibrium temperature.

In increasing from perhaps 280 ppmv (parts per million by volume) in pre-industrial times to 380 ppmv now, carbon dioxide has already produced 75 per cent of the theoretical warming that would be caused by a doubling from pre-industrial 280 to 560 ppmv. As we move from 380 to 560 ppm, at most a few tenths of a degree of warming remain in the system. Claims of greater warming rely for example on assumptions that all feedbacks are positive – statistically unlikely, probably untrue for low cloud formation, and counter to the circumstantial evidence of life having survived several billion years. However empiricism now tells us that there has been no warming for ten years during which CO_2 has risen steadily from 368 to 386 ppmv[17] – there is an almost irrefutable suspicion that CO_2 cannot be the principle driver.

An inconvenient untruth

We saw in Chapter 10 that the industrial and political determination to deploy wind power at all costs has encouraged a great deal of misrepresentation. Much the same can be said of climate change and just one example is recounted here as an indictment of this corruption of science.

In 1990, the IPCC's 1st Assessment Report[18] included a graph of the global temperature history from AD 1000 to 1990. Between 1000 and about 1400 the Medieval Warm Period (MWP) was depicted with a highest temperature much exceeding that of the modern warm period. It also showed temperature plunging to a similar degree below the present warmth to give us the Little Ice Age which terminated not long before the twentieth century. This diagram was derived from the work of distinguished climatologist, Hubert Lamb, the founder of the UEA Climate Research Unit.

In 2006 Dr David Deming of the University of Oklahoma gave testimony to the US Senate Committee on Environment & Public Works[19] that, after he had published a paper on borehole temperature historical data in *Science*, he received an email from a major researcher in the area of climate change which said, "We have to get rid of the Medieval Warm Period".

And indeed someone did. In 1999, Michael Mann and his colleagues published a reconstruction of past temperature from AD 1000 to the present, in which the MWP simply vanished. This unique estimate became known as the "hockey stick," because of the shape of the temperature graph. The long straight shaft represented unchanging temperature from 1000 to the beginning of the modern warming, taking-off into the future as the sharp upward angle of the blade. By the time of the IPCC's 3rd Assessment Report in 2001[20] the hockey-stick and the very similar graph of CO_2 during the same period had become the trademark of global warming, featuring in hundreds of presentations and press reports as scientifically illiterate "proof" that CO_2 was warming the earth. The diagrams were included several times in the main 3rd Assessment Report and also as large illustrations in the *Summary for Policymakers*.

There is not space here to explain what happened next but careful investigation revealed that the hockey-stick had been created by a statistical manipulation which, by over-weighting parts of the data set could create the hockey-stick shape from any – even a random data set. Amidst protestations of outrage and innocence the diagrams have quietly disappeared from prominence and no longer feature in the IPCC's 4th Assessment Report SPM[21] nor as "convincing" slides in presentations. With the loss of the hockey stick, the MWP has been recreated and there is no doubt from the historical record and proxy data that it was at least as warm as the present day despite our "unprecedentedly high CO_2". Similarly the Little Ice Age is even better documented as colder than the present and recovery from it was certainly the beginning of recent warming triggered by what? Certainly not man-made CO_2.

Carbon dioxide may or may not play an important role in controlling global temperature but other factors must be involved and are the more likely cause of the sudden warming and cooling events which we have seen on a small scale in modern times and through prehistory as the cyclic oscillation of glacial and interglacial periods. Cyclic changes in solar radiant flux have long been recognised as driving the glacial resurgences but as to the shorter term events like the temperature hiatus of 1940 to 1970 or now in the last decade, we do not as yet know and claims that mathematical models can tell us the answers are simply untrue and as we have just seen, encourage intellectual recklessness or was it dishonesty?

References and notes

1. Jean Baptiste Joseph, Baron de Fourier, in 1807, suggested that the earth's atmosphere acts like the glass of a hothouse. *Theorie Analytique de la Chaleur*. The concept may be even older.

2. Beck, E.-G. (2007) 180 Years of Atmospheric CO_2 Gas Analysis by Chemical Methods. *Energy & Environment* Volume 18 No. 2. Beck re-examined a large number of early volumetric and titrimetric analyses of CO_2, concluding that concentrations have not been so stable with time as other modern workers have assumed.

3. R.F. Keeling et al. Atmospheric Carbon Dioxide Record from Mauna Loa 1958-2007 http://cdiac.ornl.gov/trends/co2/sio-mlo.html

4. Report of the Conference of the Parties on its Third Session, Held at Kyoto From 1 to 11 December, 1997. Addendum Part Two: Action Taken by the Conference of the Parties at its Third Session.

5. Hadley Centre for Climate Prediction and Research (Meteorological Office) http://www.cru.uea.ac.uk/cru/data/temperature/hadcrut3gl.txt

6. Gray, V. (2006) Temperature trends in the lower atmosphere. *Energy & Environment 17*, 707-714

7. International Geoscience Programme (IGCP) Project 512: Neoproterozoic Ice Ages http://www.igcp512.org/.

8. Monnin et al. (2001)`Atmospheric CO_2 Concentrations over the Last Glacial Termination. *Science*, vol.291, p.112. Shows a time lag of 800 years.

9. IPCC (2000) Draft WG1 Third Assessment Report Chapter 14. The quotation which is obviously crucial and just as true today was in a

section on chaos in climatology and omitted from the *Summary for Policymakers*.

10. IPCC (2002) *Special Report on Emission Scenarios* (SRES).

11. Fischer, H et al. (1999) Ice Core Records of Atmospheric CO_2 Around the Last Three Glacial Terminations. *Science*, 283, 1712 – 1714.

12. Etherington J. R. (1975) *Environment and Plant Ecology* 1st edn John Wiley.

13. IPCC (2001) *Third Assessment Report. Summary for Policymakers*. The IPCC's future "scenarios" (its word) for projected climate are largely based on mathematical models which effectively deliver century-long weather forecasts.

14. IPCC (2007) *4th Assessment Report. Summary for Policymakers*.

15. Lindzen et al. (2001) Does the Earth have an Adaptive Infrared Iris? *Bull. American Meteorological Society* 82 417-32.

16. Spencer, R. (2007) Cirrus disappearance: Warming might thin heat-trapping clouds. University of Alabama, Huntsville. Earth System Science Center press release.

17. Mauna Loa CO_2 record. Scripps Institution of Oceanography, National Oceanic and Atmospheric Administration. ftp://ftp.cmdl.noaa.gov/ccg/co2/trends/co2_mm_mlo.txt

18. IPCC (2007) *1st Assessment Report*.

19. U.S. Senate Committee on Environment & Public Works Hearing Statements (12/06/2006). Statement of Dr David Deming, University of Oklahoma http://epw.senate.gov/hearing_statements.cfm?id=266543

20. See 13.

21. See 14.

12 Epilogue

We will need a mix of both onshore and offshore wind energy to meet the UK's challenging targets on climate change. (BWEA[1])

It is hard to believe that a man is telling the truth when you know that you would lie if you were in his place. (H L Mencken)

Wind power as we have seen fails in a whole list of criteria.

It cannot provide a predictable electricity supply at the click of a switch. Consequently it would not be marketable without an obligation to purchase – a bitter pill which is sweetened by an enormous subsidy.

It was initially sold to the public as preventing emission of CO_2. In fact it saves a remarkably small amount, which has been grossly exaggerated, as the industry has been humiliatingly forced to admit. The need for backup has been ignored in the carbon-accounting by all but a few multinational energy companies with experience of very large-scale wind power operation.

As a supplier of electricity and a mitigation of carbon emission it is remarkably expensive, in particular because each megawatt-worth of installed capacity and transmission line produces or carries not much more than a quarter of that output because of the wind-limited load factor. In due course, dedicated backup will be required but will be unable to cover its own costs as by definition it must be standing-by and not generating electricity for much of the time.

It has a huge landscape footprint for a tiny but costly contribution to electricity supply – often 300 to 400 km^2 of visual impact for no more than a few megawatts of wobbly power.

The RO subsidy in the UK has however made wind power an attractive investment for multinationals with the financial backing to carry the initial capital expenditure and indeed, in all countries the unprecedented subsidy has driven a culture of bullying, misrepresentation and occasionally law-breaking. For example whilst writing these final words, the following appeared:

> Italy police arrest 8 in Mafia wind farms plot. Operation "Aeolus," named after the ancient Greek god of winds, netted eight suspects, arrested in the Trapani area of western Sicily [and on the Italian mainland]. Police in Trapani said the local Mafia bribed city officials in nearby Mazara del Vallo so the town would invest in wind farms to produce energy. (Associated Press, 2009 [Google hosted])

Truth and even legality have come to grief in this industry. It is very apparent that with unlimited sums of money for a nearly invisible product, what else shall we grow but a mafia-culture?

This damning compendium of failure suggests that we would be better off without wind power at all – that is certainly my view, but it has been part of the successful strategy of the wind power industry to represent any opposition as being both negative and misled. Thus I feel no more compelling need to suggest an "alternative" to wind than I would offer in exchange for the fairies at the bottom of my garden, pedalling their infinite power generator!

However my editor says this seems negative so, to avoid being branded anarchic, I offer the following, hopefully acceptable to all sides (unlikely!), but as we are looking for an "alternative" to an ailing horse, the finishing post may be one which many would rather not see.

I start with an elimination exercise. To be acceptable, a power generating technology must:

1. Provide a secure supply of electricity – that is, be available to order.
2. Provide a substantial and preferably unlimited percentage of generation.
3. Save substantial CO_2 emission as a cost-effective way of fulfilling the original justification – that of displacing fossil carbon fuel – now cleverly and dishonestly summed up in the PR phrase, "tackling climate change".
4. Not require substantial backup as a proportion of achieved generating capacity (wind power needs about three times installed capacity and thermal about a quarter).
5. Not be perceived as socially unacceptable (the last two newspaper polls that I saw before writing this showed 76% and 88% against wind power – *Cambridge News* 27.3.09 and *Carmarthen Journal* 1.4.09!).

Wind completely fails on all of these counts, so what other options are there?

Option 1. Wind fails to give secure supply so, because it needs substantial thermal back-up let us just build more coal-fired or gas-fired power stations and not bother with the wind at all.

Unacceptable politically because of the Russian finger on the gas tap (or that of the Middle East, which the West has deeply offended of recent years). In any case, if we use coal or gas there is failure to "tackle climate change" and environmental problems are posed by the extractive industries.

Option 2. Let's use coal, fitted with carbon capture and storage (CCS), thus securing a UK fuel supply for a century or more and also addressing the climate problem if it exists.

Unacceptable because CCS has not been tested on more than a mini-scale, financed by CO_2-enhanced oil recovery. It is not known to work in the long term and the prospect of many billions of tonnes of liquid CO_2 corroding its way out of a geological tomb is a disturbing thought. The US has just announced that their most ambitious CCS programme has collapsed because of cost.[3] In the UK CCS will be even more expensive and problem-fraught because it needs sub-sea disposal. Also, it is strongly opposed by the green lobby as deliberately encouraging use of fossil fuel. Recently, the Greenpeace protestors against coal-firing and CCS at Kingsnorth power station in Kent were effectively forgiven their law-breaking by a judge who urged the jury to accept that it was in the "public interest". This precedent bodes ill for rational decision-taking.

Option 3. Other renewable. This is an unacceptable way forward at least for the 2010 and 2020 targets as there are no other renewables available to the UK which are in sufficient quantity and developed enough even to scratch the problem. The choices are hydroelectricity for which there is very little remaining resource, biological fuels which are now well exploited but there is a growing and insoluble problem of land area for production. This is a pity as hydro- and biomass are the only renewables which provide firm "turn of a switch" electricity. The remaining sources pose a similar intermittency problem to wind power and have been relatively little researched or financed, not being seen as a "quick buck" investment as is wind. Tidal generation at present provides no electricity at all in the UK and wave power from a tiny experimental project is insufficient to be recorded in DBERR's *Digest of UK Energy Statistics*. Solar PV electricity needs energy storage to get over the night-time problem but might one day be a solution in high sunlight areas. It is not cost-effective in our climate where it is never likely to give a substantial supply and political attempts to force its adoption may be counterproductive, branding it a failure.

Option 4. The fourth and final option is a word which for so long could not be spoken – Nuclear.

Nuclear power could give secure supply of very large amounts of electricity with little fuel supply problem as uranium is currently sourced from politically friendly states and there is possibility of further supplies from thorium. The former Government Chief Scientific Adviser, Sir David King, told Government that 40% from nuclear was a suitable target but there seems no practical reason why the UK could not emulate France and have up to 80% of its generation provided in this way, massively satisfying the climate change requirement as there is next to no CO_2 emission.

The green organisations are in a dilemma – needing to decide which is worse – CO_2 or the threat of radioactive materials. A few notable green campaigners have already grasped this glowing nettle.

The four leading environmentalists who are now lobbying in favour of nuclear power are Stephen Tindale, former director of Greenpeace; Lord Chris Smith of Finsbury, the chairman of the Environment Agency; Mark Lynas, author of the Royal Society's science book of the year, and Chris Goodall, a Green Party activist and prospective parliamentary candidate.[2]

Finland and France are currently building 1,600 MW nuclear stations of the AREVA EPR pressurized water design. All nuclear power is best suited to constant peak running, thus providing baseload power. Even now with many closures behind us, nuclear in the UK still provides a considerable proportion of the baseload supply. However, unlike our present nuclear fleet of old Magnox reactors and Advanced Gas-cooled reactors (AGRs), the new Pressurised Water Reactor (PWR) stations would permit load-following operation if necessary.

As we have seen, wind power can fill neither of these roles but simply supplies bulk MWh when the wind is available, unrelated to night and day variation in demand or peak demands caused by the weather or TV-break kettles.

Thus, by elimination and, like it or not, nuclear satisfies every demand of a power system and it also "tackles climate change", if saving CO_2 emission is truly necessary. It also conserves fossil fuel which will always be required in limited quantity for specialist processes and as chemical feedstock. And of course one EPR station is equivalent to over 2,500 big wind turbines!

In the wind power debate we have been repeatedly bullied into silence as nuclear power could not be mentioned without its being used as a smear – something discreditably akin to a perversion. I admit to having succumbed to this bullying – rarely mentioning the subject except to demolish the untruthful "Rather have wind than nuclear" – a common scare tactic in the mouths of politicians and the media, which I mention in Chapter 10.

The bottom line in this process of elimination is that we have allowed ourselves to be delayed so long by green opposition that nuclear power could not now be deployed in time to avert a crisis (the building time will be 10-15 years). To overcome the looming energy crisis only gas CCGTs can be up and running on a four or five year time scale (already several big ones are permitted and others are "in the pipeline"). Just pray that Mr Putin and the Arab nations don't get really annoyed with us in the meantime.

What is even more disturbing is that the delay imposed by the green organisations and the belief in renewables with which they seduced so many politicians, not only forces us into a politically untenable position but also may result in a rush for nuclear as wind power is recognised for the "scam" that it is. This will lead to a dangerously hasty decision process in the very industry where extra care is needed and also sets back our position in the queue for design and construction expertise which retirement and death has already radically whittled down in our own power industry.

The green organisations and the politicians carry almost entire blame for a situation in which failing wind power has been presented as an only option to achieve entirely symbolic targets. I for one have no wish to see my beautiful country marred by many thousands of twitching crucifixions of landscape for such little return that the yearly operation of one Boeing 747 airliner negates the entire carbon displacement by several large wind farms.[4] At the same time politicians insult my intelligence by ludicrous claims that their numerous flights are being "offset" by tree-planting and that it is socially unacceptable that I oppose the "tackling of climate change" by wind power – a patent impossibility.

I cannot find words better than geologist, Malcolm Rider's:

> The Highlands are being humiliated by wind farm developers who insist they are saving the environment. They lie; they are here to make a profit. Wind farms produce very little and intermittent electricity. Most of the time they do not work. How can the blade of a bulldozer ripping up 6,000 years of beautifully preserved archaeology be saving the environment? How can the turbine blades smashing a golden eagle to bits be saving the environment? How can the government of Scotland destroy such a prize? And use public money to do it?[5]

References and notes

1. BWEA Website *Top Myths about Wind Energy*.
2. *The Independent* (23 February 2009) Nuclear power? Yes please . . .
3. *Nature* (19 March, 2009) Vol 458. US government's flagship 'clean coal' plant, FutureGen, was to have captured and stored 90% of its carbon dioxide emissions.
4. In 2002 I wrote, "a single 747 Jumbo jet flying over the proposed Cefn Croes wind power station, spewing out CO_2 faster than Cefn Croes could save it" (*Western Mail*, 12 March, 2002). By 2005 more accurate information allowed George Monbiot to claim "One daily connection between Britain and Florida costs three giant wind farms." Later corroboration was given in Views of Scotland Briefing Paper 6, October 2007 *Carbon savings and wind power on Lewis*.
5. Rider, M. (2009) *Hutton's Arse*. Rider-French Consulting Ltd.

Glossary of Abbreviations and Acronyms

ADT – Advanced Digital Tracker system
AGR – advanced gas-cooled reactor
AM – aerodynamic modulation
AONB – Areas of Outstanding Natural Beauty
AREVA EPR – French multinational mainly known for nuclear power
ASA – Advertising Standards Authority
ATS – air traffic services
AWEA – American Wind Energy Association
BERR see DBERR
BP – Before Present
BWEA – British Wind Energy Association
CAA – Civil Aviation Authority
CCGT – Combined cycle gas turbine station
CCL – Climate Change Levy
CCLe – Climate Change Levy exemption
CCS – carbon capture and storage
CEC – California Energy Commission
CERT – Carbon Emissions Reduction Target
CHP – combined heat and power
CLOWD – Campaign to Limit Onshore Windfarm Development
CPRW – Campaign for the Protection of Rural Wales
CWIF – Caithness Windfarm Information Forum
dB – Decibel
DBERR/BERR – Department of Business, Enterprise and Regulatory Reform (UK Government) formerly DTI
DECC – Department of Energy and Climate Change (UK Government)
DEFRA – Department for Environment, Food, and Rural Affairs (UK Government)

DENA – Deutsche Energie-Agentur GmbH – German Energy Agency

DTI – Department of Trade and Industry (UK Government) now DBERR

DUKES – Digest of UK Energy Statistics

DWIA – Danish Wind Industry Association

EAP – Energy Advisory Panel (DTI)

E.On UK – subsidiary of E.ON Nnetz (formerly PowerGen)

E.ON Nnetz – German based power company

EC – European Community

EDF – Electricité de France (EDF Energy)

EIA – Environment Impact Assessment

EPR – European Pressurised Reactor

ERC – see UK ERC

ESB – Electricity Supply Board

ETSU-R-97 Wind farm noise guidelines (UK) [Working Group on Noise from Wind Turbines]

ETSU – Energy Technology Support Unit (DTI)

EU – European Union

GHG – Greenhouse gas

HAWT – horizontal axis wind turbines

IPC – Infrastructure Planning Commission

IPCC – UN Intergovernmental Panel on Climate Change

KIA – Kent International Airport

LIA – Little Ice Age

LOS – Line of sight

LPA – Local Planning Authorities

MAIWAG – Marton, Askam & Ireleth Windfarm Action Group

MOD/MoD – Ministry of Defence

MRET – Mandatory Renewable Energy Target (Australia)

MWP – Medieval Warm Period

NATS – National Air Traffic Service

NFFO – Non Fossil Fuel Obligation, see RO

NETA – New Electricity Trading Arrangements

NNR – National Nature Reserves

NA – Noise Association

NPPG and SPP – National Planning Policy Guideline (Scotland)

OCGT – Open circuit gas turbine generation
Ofgem – Office of Gas and Electricity Markets
PAC – Public Accounts Committee of the House of Commons
PPS – Planning Policy Statement (England)
PSR – Primary surveillance radar
PWR station – Pressurised Water Reactor
REF – Renewable Energy Foundation
RES – Renewable Energy Systems
RICS – Royal Institution of Chartered Surveyors
RICS-OBS survey - with Oxford-Brookes University
RO – Renewables Obligation (former NFFO – Non-fossil Fuel Obligation)
ROC – Renewables Obligation Certificate
RPS – State Renewable Portfolio Standard (US)
RSPB – Royal Society for the Protection of Birds
RTE – Radio Telefis Eireann
RWE npower – German-based power company
SAC – Special Areas of Conservation
SHWAG – Seamer & Hilton Windfarm Action Group
SDC – Sustainable Development Commission
SNH – Scottish National Heritage
SPA – Special Protection Areas
SRES Special Report on Emission Scenarios
SSA – Strategic Search Areas
SSSI – Sites of Special Scientific Interest
TAN – Technical Advice Note (Wales)
TSO – Transmission system operators
UCTE – Union for the Co-ordination of Transmission of Electricity
UKERC – UK Energy Research Centre
UNEP – United Nations Environment Programme
VAD – Vibroacoustic Disease
VAWT – vertical axis wind turbines
WMO – World Meteorological Organization
WT – wind turbines
WTB – Wales Tourist Board
WTG Wind turbine generators

Index